Second European Regional Conference
Geneva   January 1974

Report II

Some Growing Employment Problems in Europe

Second item on the agenda

Manpower Aspects of Recent Economic Developments in Europe

International
Labour
Office
Geneva

ISBN 92-2-101028-7

First published 1973

ILO publications can be obtained through major booksellers or ILO local offices in many countries, or direct from ILO Publications, International Labour Office, CH-1211 Geneva 22, Switzerland. The catalogue and list of booksellers and local offices will be sent free of charge from the above address.

Printed by International Labour Office, Geneva

TABLE OF CONTENTS

INTRODUCTION

This report concentrates on three main topics within the employment field - topics which were selected because they were held to be growing in urgency and calling for early, concerted action by European countries.

The first concerns the implications for the average European's working career of recent changes in the nature of employment and the characteristics of the labour force, and of the shift in educational thinking towards the concept of life-long education.[1] Here it is suggested that new and more flexible patterns of working life would not only open up greater freedom of choice for the individual but might assist in the adjustment of the labour force to the changing trends of the labour market (Chapter II).

The second concerns the employment problems connected with the rapid expansion of formal higher education, much of which is taking place without sufficient regard to the employment opportunities that will be open to students following graduation and during their working lives (Chapter III).

The third concerns the place of international migration in the employment policies both of sending and receiving countries. In some places, problems are reaching crisis proportions, or will shortly do so if present trends continue. Chapter IV seeks to analyse the problems and to come up with some suggestions as to lines along which the countries concerned might jointly seek solutions. Most of the Socialist countries are less involved in international migration, but brief reference is made in the chapter to their experience.

In order to place these three topics in their setting, they have been preceded by a first chapter which looks very rapidly at changes in the employment scene which took place in the last decade. Comparative statistical tables illustrating some of these changes have been brought together in the Statistical Appendix.

Finally, Chapter V suggests, on the basis of the earlier chapters, what themes the Conference might wish to discuss.

----

[1] As reflected in the conclusions of the International Commission on the Development of Education (the Edgar Faure Commission): Learning_to_be:__the_world_of__education__today and_tomorrow (Paris, UNESCO; London, Harrap), 1972.

CHAPTER I

THE_GENERAL_EMPLOYMENT_BACKGROUND

Before approaching the specialised themes of this report, it is useful to take a rapid look at the broad sweep of change which took place in Europe between 1960 and 1970 in the size and composition of the labour force; in the distribution of employment; in the level and nature of unemployment; in the type of manpower problems besetting countries; and in policies for dealing with these problems.

Quantitative_aspects

Growth_of_the_labour_force

The revised labour force projections issued by the International Labour Office in 1971[1] put the annual growth rate of the labour force of Europe (excluding USSR) at 0.66 per cent from 1960 to 1965 and at only 0.51 per cent from 1965 to 1970; in 1970 to 1975, the annual growth rate will rise to 0.62 per cent, but will drop again in 1975 to 1980 to 0.54 per cent. This means that, from 1965 to 1980, the labour force of this region is growing at less than one-third of the rate of the labour force of the world as a whole. The labour force of the USSR as a whole (the figures include the Asian as well as European parts of the Union) is growing more than twice as fast as that of the rest of Europe, but the rate is still below the world average (for purposes of comparison, it may be interesting to note also that it is below that for Northern America) and there are regions within the Union where the rate is as low as in the rest of Europe.

Europe as a whole is thus fortunate in not having to cope with the most intractable manpower problem which faces the developing continents: that of the rapid growth of the labour force outstripping the pace at which new employment opportunities arise.[2] Compared with the other major areas of the world, Europe is not compelled to place priority on
----

[1] Labour_force__projections,__1965-1985 (Geneva, ILO), 1971, in particular Part V, World Summary.

[2] See table 1 in the Statistical Appendix to this report. This shows, inter_alia, that from 1975 to 1980, the labour force of Latin America and the Caribbean will be growing almost five times as fast as that of Europe (excl. USSR).

absolute employment growth solely to absorb new additions to the labour force; it can devote more resources per head to education and training; and it can give more attention to the qualitative factors of employment. Moreover, where employment growth is called for, the inputs needed in the form of capital and skills are mostly available in reasonable quantities.

This is not to deny the existence of problems of employment growth in parts of Europe (some of these continue to be troublesome) but to suggest that, seen through Latin American, Asian or African eyes, they appear to be ones which the European countries, in a spirit of co-operation, should be able to solve and still have thought left over for the employment difficulties of the developing continents.

There are of course considerable variations in labour force growth rates from one European country to another.[1] The rates range from negative ones in Austria and the German Democratic Republic in 1960-70 to an annual growth rate of 2.2 per cent in Turkey in 1970-80.[2] Poland maintains a consistently high rate of growth and the Netherlands and Yugoslavia also have rates well above the average. On the other hand, Hungary, Malta, Portugal and the United Kingdom will have, during the current decade, a labour force which is scarcely, if at all, growing.

Have either the low rates of labour force growth or the high rates raised problems for the countries concerned?

It is clear that the Federal Republic of Germany would have been unable to achieve its high rates of economic growth if it had had to rely exclusively on its national labour force; within the Soviet Union, continued difficulty is experienced in finding sufficient manpower for Siberia and the Far East regions of the RSFSR, where the great mineral and energy reserves are located[3]; and it also seems likely that the German Democratic Republic and Hungary have been hampered to some extent by the stagnation of their labour force. But elsewhere if there have been bottlenecks in economic growth due to manpower shortage, they have more

----

[1] See table 2 in the Statistical Appendix, which gives the projections for twenty-seven European countries.

[2] Turkey is in fact the one European country with a major quantitative employment problem comparable to that of developing countries in other continents and it is, significantly, the one European country which has requested advice under the World Employment Programme.

[3] Between 1959 and 1970, there was an actual population outflow from Siberian regions and certain localities of the Far East, and this is leading in turn to a drastic decline in the birth rate.

often been ascribed to specific shortages of skills, or to lack of mobility in the labour force than to deficiency in the total numbers. As regards the future, the United Kingdom for example shows little concern about the minimal growth of its labour force and expects to achieve its economic targets without additions to its labour force through immigration. In some cases, low labour force growth has in practice stimulated higher participation rates and striking increases in labour productivity; contrariwise, in some countries it is argued that the free availability of migrant workers in the latter half of the 1950s and in the 1960s has retarded this reaction.

The high rate of labour force growth poses a formidable problem for Turkey. Its new five-year development plan estimates that, out of about 480,000 joining the labour force annually, only 160,000 are able to enter productive activities; that on current trends, unemployment is likely to continue to rise till 1987,and that, between 1973 and 1995 it will be necessary to create 13 to 14 million new jobs.

For countries like Turkey (and, to a lesser extent, Yugoslavia), the situation is aggravated by the mass exodus from the rural areas which is taking place at the same time. Both countries have been thankful for the temporary safety valve of emigration (in this connection it may be remarked that Poland and Romania are accepting a considerable challenge in aiming at promoting sufficient employment both for additions to the labour force and for those no longer needed in agriculture so as not to have recourse to emigration).

As will be discussed in Chapter IV, international migration, though it can temporarily relieve problems of fast labour force growth in sending countries and of slow labour force growth in receiving countries, is not a simple matter of evening out differences in over-all labour supply; and the longer-term difficulties which international migration raises both for sending and receiving countries are being increasingly appreciated.

Changes in labour force participation rates

As regards labour force participation rates, the general pattern is one of declining rates for males, partially compensated by higher rates for women.[1] While there are no very significant differences from one country to another in the male rates, there remain quite striking differences in the female rates; these are generally higher in Eastern than in Western Europe; and within Western Europe, the Netherlands and Norway stand out as countries
----

[1] See table 3 in the Statistical Appendix.

still with low female rates (due largely to many women
withdrawing from the labour market definitively on marriage
or on the arrival of their first child).

Actual recorded changes from 1960 to 1970 in
participation rates for women in the 20-24, 25-29, 30-49 age
groups (the child-bearing and child-rearing years), for 11
countries[1] show striking increases in the propensity of
women in these age groups to go out to work; while this is
more noticeable in the Socialist countries, it is a general
trend (with the exception perhaps of Italy, where the
participation rate of married women appears to be affected
very strongly by conjunctural changes in labour demand).

Changes in sectoral distribution of employment

It is in the sectoral distribution of employment that
some of the most significant changes have been taking
place.[2]

There has been continuation of the steep decline in
employment in agriculture in all the countries listed, with
the proportion in the United Kingdom sinking below 3 per
cent[3] and in Belgium below 5 per cent.

In several countries - Belgium, Netherlands, Sweden,
Switzerland, the United Kingdom - the proportion of the
labour force in industrial employment or even the absolute
numbers in industrial employment also showed a decline.
During the decade, Belgium, Denmark, the Netherlands, Sweden
and the United Kingdom joined the United States and Canada
in wha in what has been described as the post-industrial era
- a situation in which more workers are employed in the
services sector than in the other sectors combined. In the
Socialist countries, there has also been a noticeable rise
in the previous relatively low percentages of workers in the
services sector, reflecting changes in planning goals.

Changes in employment status

In the market economies, the long-term trend for the
number of self-employed and family workers to decline, and
----

[1] See table 4 in the Statistical Appendix.

[2] Table 5 in the Statistical Appendix lists the
percentages of workers employed respectively in agriculture,
industry and services in twenty-four European countries.

[3] It has been forecast that this proportion will drop to
1.2 per cent or 1.3 per cent by 1980, at which level it is
estimated that it will just suffice to achieve production
targets; this is based on the assumption that there will be
no increase in the rate of decline of wage-paid workers.

for the number of salaried and wage-paid workers to increase
has continued.[1] This is of course related to the decline of
the number of persons in agriculture, in which these forms
of employment status are particularly prevalent; but the
same phenomenon is occurring in industry, in retail trade
and in other services. The only exception was in the United
Kingdom, which for many years has had the lowest proportion
in Western Europe of its labour force in own-account
employment; here there was a very small rise in the number
of self-employed. This may suggest that there is an
irreducible minimum below which this proportion is unlikely
to fall in a market economy (in this case just over 7 per
cent of the labour force) or it may merely be a response to
fiscal measures which tended, in certain occupations, to
favour those in self-employment.

In four Socialist countries for which comparable data
are available, there has also been a growth in the
proportion of the labour force in salaried and wage-paid
employment, as well as a move of self-employed and family
workers into production co-operatives.[2]

Changes_in_levels_of_unemployment

In the last four to five years, concern has been felt
on many occasions about the appearance in some European
market economies of unemployment rates considerably above
those for the period 1960-1966. These higher rates have
persisted for several years with the result that some
observers have gone so far as to express fears of the re-
emergence of the mass unemployment of the 1930s.
Fortunately, these fears have proved unfounded, and the
latest figures in 1973 show a downward trend in the numbers
of registered unemployed and an improved demand for workers
reflected in a higher number of vacancies notified to the
public employment service. Nevertheless, in some regions
and among some groups of the population, the index of
unemployment has remained for too long at an unacceptably
high level which cannot be regarded as consistent with a
policy of full employment; the average duration of
unemployment for certain categories of workers has
lengthened; and there are signs that, even with a return to
high levels of economic activity, a higher level of residual
unemployment may persist.

There is no discernible uniform pattern in the trend
of unemployment in the different countries for which

----

[1] See table 6A in the Statistical Appendix.

[2] See table 6B in the Statistical Appendix.

reasonably comparable date exist.[1] For instance, though the level went up simultaneously in a number of countries in 1967, the tempo of recovery (or deterioration) thereafter was very different. And there are significant exceptions. Switzerland maintained its virtual immunity from unemployment, while Austria and Norway brought their levels down below those of 1960-1966.

A glance at the more detailed national statistics (not summarised in the Appendix) shows considerable variations in the composition of the unemployed. In some countries the incidence of unemployment is highest amongst the young, in others amongst older age groups; in some among women, while in others women have a low incidence of unemployment. It is therefore unwise to attempt to generalise from the total figures, particularly as they are not comparable from one country to another owing to the different methods by which they are collected and the different concepts and criteria used.

In the last few years there have been many criticisms of the unemployment statistics currently published, some arguing that they understate the situation, others that they exaggerate it. The former point out for instance that figures based on unemployment registrations exclude those people, particularly married women, who do not bother to register; the latter that the figures, whether based on registrations or on labour force sample surveys, include people who do not necessarily all form part of a genuine labour reserve, such as those with a short waiting period between jobs. It has also been remarked in the United Kingdom that the uninformed person who reads that the total number of unemployed stays at say 750,000 for two successive months has a mental picture of the same 750,000 remaining unemployed, when in fact perhaps some 300,000 to 400,000 may have entered employment in each month, with another 300,000 to 400,000 becoming unemployed during the same period; also, some may lose one job and find another within the month without being counted at all. It is only once the unemployment total is broken down into detail by age, sex, region, duration, industry, occupation, reasons for leaving the last job, other sources of family income, etc. - and is analysed by flows as well as by static counts that its real significance can be appreciated and can provide a guide to the action needed.

In Belgium, the second session of the tripartite National Conference on Employment in April 1973 considered that analysis of the unemployment situation could not be complete without information also on migration and long-distance commuting attributable to lack of jobs, on low

---

[1] See table 7 giving annual average levels of unemployment from 1960 to 1971 reported by eighteen countries.

female participation rates and on retention of workers in low-productivity employment.

In several cases the authorities are perplexed by the persistence of higher levels of unemployment despite energetic measures which in former years would have sufficed to correct the situation. It is evident that quite satisfactory rates of economic growth have not brought the reductions in unemployment which would have been expected in the past. Many different factors leading to these higher residual levels have been suggested: declining rates of new investment in the types of industry which would create new employment; declining international competitivity of some European industries not being compensated by expansion of other industries; increased cost-consciousness of managements leading to their looking very closely at the size of their work force; mergers resulting in the closing down of less profitable or loss-making establishments and in the cutting-down of administrative staff; stoppages of work which bring secondary unemployment in their wake; increasing mismatch between vacancies and the unemployed job-seekers available to fill them, with the result that in some cases a growing demand for workers has not resulted in a significant decline in numbers of the unemployed; higher unemployment benefits and redundancy payments which allow unemployed persons to take longer over their job-search than in past years; and many others. In some cases, part of the higher level of reported unemployment may be "statistical" and not represent any real deterioration of the employment situation; for instance in Sweden, successful efforts to attract more women into the labour force raised unemployment figures at the same time as employment ones and in France new confidence in the public employment service led to increased registrations.

The United Kingdom Government, though it has not been able to isolate the causes, has remarked that a given level of unemployment now seems to correspond to a rather higher pressure of demand on resources than was previously the case.[1] This suggests that the residual unemployment remaining after traditional remedial measures have been taken is now likely to be greater than it used to be. In Sweden also, the National Labour Market Board, in presenting its budget proposals for the fiscal year 1973-74, observed that it was symptomatic of current structural changes that there was a growing disparity between vacancies and unemployed persons; during a boom with a large surplus demand for labour, a considerable proportion remained unemployed, while during a recession (with high unemployment

----

[1] A number of different explanations have however been put forward by academic research workers; see D.T. Llewellyn and P. Newbold: "The behaviour of unemployment and unfilled vacancies", Industrial Relations (Nottingham), Vol. 4, No. 1, Spring 1973.

by Swedish standards) a large number of vacancies remained
unfilled; it suggested that, consequently, the present
measures of labour market policy could not be expected to
yield the low unemployment rates of the sixties. Employers
in several countries complain of continued difficulty, even
in areas of statistically high unemployment, in finding
workers in certain categories. It seems that manpower
shortages and manpower surpluses co-exist to a greater
extent than in the past. In regard to the six original
members of the European Communities, the Commission has
remarked that in 1972 it was not proving possible to offset
the one against the other to any great extent, despite
stronger economic and social measures. This was attributed
in part to the lack of specific skills and in part to the
work being unattractice to labour which is in theory
available.[1]

Whatever the causes (and in some countries perhaps not
enough effort goes to identifying the causes and assessing
their relative importance) it seems that the remedies which
kept unemployment low in the years 1960-66 have lost some of
their bite. The release of purchasing power with a view to
increasing private consumption has not done much to promote
new jobs in the places where they are most needed, except
after a considerable time lag; industrial investment
incentives in regions of high unemployment have been less
effective at a time when industry did not generally wish to
expand its bases, or if it did so, was more often interested
in establishing capital-intensive new facilities. It has
been realised that much more selective programmes are
needed, directed more purposefully at absorbing the specific
types of unemployed worker in the area concerned. This is
not easy, but is engaging the attention of planning
authorities, both national and regional.

In those countries still experiencing an unacceptably
high level of unemployment in the earlier part of 1973 (such
as Belgium, France, Ireland, Italy and the United Kingdom)
a major cause remained the long-standing problem of regional
imbalance. Regional development policies are having some
effect, and without them the situation would undoubtedly be
more serious, but it is difficult to point to any examples
of regional development measures which have successfully
brought the level of unemployment in afflicted regions down
to the national average. There has for this reason been a
switch of interest from traditional regional development
measures to new types of measures, such as the outright
subsidisation of employment, which will have a more direct
effect in creating jobs for those who need them. There has
also been a rebirth of interest in relief-work measures,
though in more diversified forms than that of traditional
public works projects.
----

[1] Commission of the European Communities: Report on the
development of the social situation in the Community in
1972, Brussels-Luxembourg, February 1973.

Aside from its immediate effect on those who lose their jobs or on new entrants who cannot find jobs, unemployment has an unsettling effect on those in employment. The increasing discussion in the mass media of employment, redundancy and unemployment questions tends to heighten this sense of insecurity which, though it has always been a fact of life for many manual workers and lower-paid non-manual workers, is something new to others. Improved social security, though it removes much of the basis for financial fears, is not enough; self-confidence and self-respect are also involved.

The anxiety thus engendered makes it more difficult to carry out the necessary structural changes in the economy. It is clear that a reduction of the remaining unemployment is needed, not only as an end in itself, but in order to create the right climate for the inevitable further structural changes which lie ahead.

Qualitative aspects - some of the major current problems and policies for dealing with them

Adjustment to structural change

There is generally wider understanding than say five years ago of the inevitability of further structural changes in employment - and consequently of the need for more mobility of the labour force.

However, relatively few people like facing major changes in their employment (unless these are going to bring them obvious benefits) and fewer still appreciate the prospect that structural change may ease them out of employment entirely. Increased mobility is only acceptable if it is accompanied by increased employment security. This is easier said than done.

The difficulty of reconciling the two aims is well expressed in a document of the Commission of the European Communities as follows: "Employment security can no longer be synonymous with rejection of change, any more than the needed mobility can imply permanent insecurity".[1] In France, strong emphasis was placed in the VIth Plan on the
----

[1] Commission of the European Communities: Preliminary guidelines for a Community social policy programme (Brussels, 1971), document EC-SEC(71)600. (For translator: Orientations préliminaires pour un programme de politique sociale communautaire: "La sécurité de l'emploi ne peut plus être synonyme d'immobilisme, pas davantage que la mobilité nécessaire ne peut impliquer l'insécurité permanente".)

difficulty of maintaining equilibrium in an employment market undergoing deep change. Many industries in many countries are confronted with this problem of reconciling a satisfactory degree of mobility with a satisfactory degree of employment security.

Within the manpower field, the solution which is most commonly advanced is that of much improved provision of opportunities for general training at the base, to be followed by "permanent", "continuous" (or perhaps more accurately "recurrent") training whenever there is a need for the updating or switching of skills, the latter type of opportunities being provided within the enterprise for those whose employment can continue without a break, or in government-sponsored training programmes in cases where continued employment in the old enterprise is not possible. There have been notable advances in this direction in several respects: recognition of the worker's right to training in certain circumstances; acceptance by employers and by governments of greater commitments in respect of this training and the widening of all forms of training, whether this is measured in the number of places or in the variety of types of training offered.

The reports submitted in 1971 by European governments for the general survey by the Committee of Experts on the Application of the Employment Policy Instruments provided an interesting inventory of views and measures in connection with adjustments to structural change. The general approach was that no obstacle should be put in the way of change out of fear that it might lead to disruption of employment; but that far more attention than hitherto has to be given to assisting displaced workers to train for, and be placed in, new employment, and that the individual worker should be protected against income loss or other forms of undue hardship during the changeover process. Belgium for instance referred to better forecasts of changes in the occupational needs of different sectors of the economy; France and the Federal Republic of Germany to collective agreements on employment stabilisation; the Netherlands to redundancy schemes (in cases of mergers or closures) devised under the "Merger Code" of the Social and Economic Council, and to retraining schemes both for farmers affected by the farm closure programme and for retail traders affected by changes in distribution; Ukraine to the redeployment of workers becoming available as a result of higher productivity; Spain to legislation governing the order of discharge of redundant workers according to social criteria and difficulty in obtaining new employment; Bulgaria to income maintenance for those released by change until they obtain adequate skill and employment; and Austria to compensation for redundant coal-miners to offset the shortfall in earnings while they are being retrained.

The subject of income maintenance measures to make structural change more acceptable is dealt with in detail in

Report III to this Conference; that report also describes associated developments which have occurred in labour legislation and collective agreements.

A special aspect of this subject yet to be seriously tackled is that of adjustment which would facilitate the introduction of a better international division of labour between the industrialised countries (in Europe and elsewhere) and the developing countries. The problem is well known and has been extensively discussed in the international organisations concerned with trade.[1] The current trading practices of most industrialised countries still place the highest import barriers in the way precisely of labour-intensive goods whose production, in an open world economy, would normally be taken over by the developing countries with their plentiful supplies of labour. One of the major reasons for this defensive attitude is that freer entry of such goods would entail displacement of workers whose satisfactory resettlement in other jobs would raise problems. The International Development Strategy for the Second Development Decade states in paragraph 35 that the developed countries, "having in mind the importance of facilitating the expansion of their imports from developing countries, will consider adopting measures and where possible evolving a programme early in the Decade for assisting the adaptation and adjustment of industries and workers in situations where they are adversely affected by increased imports of manufactures and semi-manufactures from developing countries". The ILO is currently carrying out a study of adjustment assistance measures of this kind taken in a number of developed market economies (including six in Europe) with a view to seeing how successful they are. It is hoped that this will suggest a combination of measures which might offer promise of coping with the adjustment problems that would result from further liberalisation of imports from developing countries.

A special problem which arises is that the workers liable to be displaced are likely to be those who would have the greatest difficulty in making the necessary adaptation to the changed labour market. Governments are looking for ways in which the necessary adaption can be shifted on to the backs of more adaptable younger workers, but this is not easy in the case, for instance, of the textile industry, which is often concentrated in areas with limited alternative employment, and which has an aging work force.

----

[1] For an interesting discussion of the issues involved here, see papers by P. Moussa, H.O. Vetter and J. Tinbergen on "Promotion of industrialization in the developing countries: implications for Community industry" in <u>Towards a European Model of Development</u>, report of a conference organised by the Commission of European Communities on industry and society in the European Community, Venice, April 1972 (Brussels, 1973).

Mismatch

Another problem to which repeated reference is made in government statements is that of "mismatch" - the failure of manpower supply to meet the requirements of available jobs, or seen the other way round, the failure of jobs to meet the aspirations of those seeking employment. This has already been noted as one of the causes of unemployment in some of the market economies, but it is a problem also in other countries and in other connections.

There are many forms of mismatch: workers are plentiful in one area but difficulty is experienced in attracting new economic activities to that area; in another area, jobs are available but workers from a distance will not move to them; jobs may be vacant for men, but only women are available, or vice versa; skilled jobs may be vacant but only unskilled applicants available; or conversely, unskilled jobs may be offered but applicants do not come forward for them because the younger generations have received more advanced education which leads them to aspire to something else.

These problems have been with us for some time and, with the vastly increased attention given in the last two decades to manpower planning and to improved guidance and training, one might have expected them to decline in importance. But that is not happening. And, in fact, a new form of mismatch has arisen (or rather, a form which has not bothered Europe since the 1930s) as a result of the expansion of higher education. In several countries, new graduates of universities have found that they are unable to obtain the type of job they expected and are having to take jobs for which a university education is not a necessary preparation. This has hit not only students of the humanities, who were to some extent forewarned of possible employment difficulties, but also scientists and technologists for whom the manpower forecasters had held out prospects of an unsatisfied demand for several years to come. This situation seems to have been the joint result of rapid expansion of higher education in response to the rising educational aspirations of young people and over-optimistic appreciation of what the effective demand of the economy for graduates would be. Unless something is done about this form of mismatch it is likely to become more serious as time goes on and as more and more young people each year reach the educational standard qualifying them for entry to higher education. The problem is examined in Chapter III.

Taking the job to the worker and the worker to the job

It has already been mentioned that existing regional development measures seem to be slow in reducing regional disparities in levels of employment (the same could be said of regional disparities in income). Nevertheless, such measures are growing in sophistication and have become an essential part of economic planning. There is no question of discontinuing them; however, their effects are longer-term than was originally thought. It would be wise therefore to recognise that any future multinational attempts to plan the regional development of large areas of Europe as a whole (as for instance within the European Communities), desirable though they are, are likely to be slow in bearing fruit. This is not an argument for giving up such measures, but on the contrary for starting them as soon as adequate planning can be completed.

There seems to have been little progress in recent years in regard to encouragement of geographical mobility of manpower within countries. In several Western European countries, government financial aids to this end have been improved, yet their utilisation does not seem to have risen much.

In the USSR, difficulty continues to be experienced in attracting good skilled workers to Eastern Siberia and the Far East and retaining them there[1], despite substantial salary and wage premiums and special provisions regarding holidays, seniority rights and social security. The policy at present is to increase the real income of workers in these regions by further wage differentials and to make the regions more attractive to live in by the construction of well-appointed housing, pre-school institutions, schools, hospitals and service enterprises; it has been estimated that expenditure on housing is likely to be the most effective means of reducing the rate of out-migration (although the average housing space available to urban residents of Siberia and the Far East has increased in recent years, housing conditions are still inferior to those in European regions of the RSFSR).

Some of the other Socialist countries which have followed a policy of decentralisation of industry to small towns or rural areas have experienced difficulty in attracting the desired calibre of qualified staff to the new establishments because of the absence of the urban amenities to which prospective candidates are accustomed. Again, the provision of amenities and of modern housing has in some cases been found to be the most effective way of attracting the persons needed. Perhaps more thought should go to incentives of this kind, though they have the potentially costly side-effect of raising the housing and amenity

----

[1] For certain top priority construction projects in these regions, manpower is obtained by appealing to the patriotic and pioneering sentiments of members of the Komsomol to go as volunteer members of construction teams; in these cases, the majority of the young people involved are reported to settle down in the regions concerned.

aspirations of existing residents. Some of the financial incentives to encourage individual geographic mobility are discussed in Report III.

In some countries, labour economists are taking the view that, in past discussions of employment mobility, the importance of the "internal labour market" has been neglected, that is, personnel movements within large undertakings having branches in different parts of the country and sometimes in different industries. Just as the supply and demand represented by the internal labour market are seldom reflected in official assessments of the employment situation, so internal mobility may not enter into official estimates of mobility.[1]

Older workers

One of the main concerns of the labour market authorities in several countries has been the resettlement of older workers thrown out of employment by closures. For many years studies have revealed the greater difficulties of older redundant workers in finding new jobs, even when they are as skilled as or more highly skilled than young redundant workers; more recently, this problem has hit older office workers and executives, who had hitherto felt reasonably secure in their employment. Though governments, employers and workers are generally in agreement with the principle that the social costs of progress should not be borne by the least competitive groups - in this case the older workers - the problem is still there. Approaches have been made to it. For instance in Spain, the Government seeks to dissuade employers from discharging workers over 40 years of age; in Sweden, the prescribed minimum period of notice now rises in length after 45 years of age, and labour market boards have been given the authority to investigate the situation in individual undertakings as regards the employment of older workers and, where appropriate, to issue directives aimed at improving the employment opportunities for older workers in the undertakings concerned; in several countries (of which Belgium may be given as an example), there are financial incentives to employers to take on older workers, such as subsidies during the initial months or relief in the payment of social security contributions. Various forms of income maintenance for the individual older worker affected by structural change are described in Report III. In Socialist countries the problem arises less

----

[1] To take an example from another continent, some large Japanese companies claim that the combination of lifelong commitment to one employer with a wide spectrum of activities carried out by that employer offers an excellent way of reconciling employment security and mobility, in that cross transfers between different types of employment are very easy to effect.

frequently, as employing establishments are normally required to carry their older workers up to the time when they are eligible for retirement pension.

A distinct question is that of older workers wishing to continue in employment after pensionable age. This is discussed in Chapter II.

Women workers

Questions relating to women workers are assuming more importance in almost all European countries. This is no doubt partly due to the increasing extent to which the economy relies on their labour. However there is also an element of recognition, long overdue, of the serious employment inequalities in practice which still face women and girls. Two types of inequalities are now getting more attention: those which spring from out-dated concepts of distinct employment roles for the two sexes, and those which derive from inadequate arrangements to help women workers with family responsibilities to fulfil their dual work and home roles.

The Scandinavian countries in particular have attempted to attack the former type of inequality at its roots by questioning all established ideas on sex roles in employment. This involves not only encouraging girls to broaden their ambitions to cover every possible type of employment and encouraging boys not to exclude occupations such as that of nursery school teacher which have hitherto been filled exclusively by women; it involved rewriting of children's reading primers to ensure that they do not sow in young children's minds stereotyped ideas as to what sort of work men do and what sort of work women do. In Sweden, proposals have even been made to subsidise the training of the other sex in occupations where one sex at present predominates and to impose a condition for the payment of training grants in development regions that neither male nor female participation should exceed 60 per cent.

As regards the second type of inequality, there has certainly been progress in recognition of the special employment problems of women with family responsibilities, and of the need for governments and employers to introduce more flexible arrangements which will permit women to move in and out of the labour force more easily, to obtain appropriate training when they need it, to work part time or flexible hours, to have special time off in the case of sickness of young children and so on. Implementation of such arrangements is however slow. Several aspects of this problem are dealt with in Chapter II.

Difficulty in filling unpopular jobs

A problem confronting socialist and market economies alike and stemming to a large extent from rising educational levels is that of the growing disaffection of workers for certain types of unskilled, heavy, dirty or otherwise unpleasant or low-status jobs, and for jobs requiring inconvenient hours of work. The jobs concerned are not the same in all countries, but it is fairly common to find that there is difficulty in recruiting persons for occupations such as labourers for brickworks, building, foundries, tanneries, hotel and restaurant kitchens, and hospitals; railway carriage, bus and car washers and public transport workers generally; nursing aides for psychiatric hospitals; night-shift workers in textile factories; automobile assembly workers, etc. In many ways this is a welcome symptom of improved living standards and of workers' greater ability than in the past to exercise freedom of choice of employment; but it will raise serious problems for the manning of these sectors, some of which are ones with constant or even growing demand for labour. For some Western European countries, the problem has been masked by the ease with which they have been able to obtain foreign workers who are prepared to accept these jobs, partly because of economic need and partly because they have lower employment aspirations resulting from their lower educational levels. By this expedient, a solution of the problem could be postponed indefinitely, since the pool of surplus and less well-educated workers in the developing continents is almost unlimited but, as will be discussed in Chapter IV, there are very serious economic and social objections to the continued influx of foreign workers into low status jobs at the present rates.

Almost all European countries will have to tackle this problem sooner or later; the Socialist countries and others which are opposed in principle to the expedient of mass admission of foreign workers for unskilled jobs may have to face it first.

The approach to this problem most commonly suggested is a combination of (a) eliminating some of these jobs through further mechanisation, (b) broadening, upgrading and humanising the remaining jobs so as to make them less unattractive, (c) letting wages rise to a level corresponding better to the scarcity value of applicants for those jobs, and (d) non-financial measures designed to raise the social status attaching to the jobs. None of these measures is easy to apply. Many of the jobs, particularly those in the services sector, do not lend themselves either to much further mechanisation or to job enrichment; there is traditional and institutional resistance in some quarters to the idea that the unskilled might earn more than the skilled; and there does not seem to be much confidence in the chances of raising the social status of these jobs. This is clearly a subject to which more attention will have to be given.

Long-term implications

More thought could also be given to the long-term implications for employment planning of a number of the other changes we have discussed - for instance, in the structure of employment and manpower requirements; in the composition and behaviour of the labour force; in the proportion of the younger population proceeding to different forms of secondary and higher education and the resulting effect on their attitude to employment; and in the role of foreign workers.

These changes dictate a more imaginative approach, particularly in relation to the moments in a person's life when he or she starts, interrupts or resumes his or her education or training; when he or she starts or stops working; when he or she chooses to take what will in future be increased spells of leisure. There is great potential flexibility in the labour force which can help the working world adjust to coming structural changes if we will only provide the means to bring it out.

CHAPTER II

ADJUSTING TO STRUCTURAL CHANGE THROUGH
NEW PATTERNS OF WORKING LIFE

The need of European economies for greater flexibility in the labour force (both quantitative and qualitative) is occurring at the same time as a growing desire among the people forming that labour force to be freed from some of the constraints which seem at present to pre-ordain their way of life and to impose irksome (and now, it seems to them, unnecessary) restrictions in the sequence of study, work and leisure.

Can these two currents be made to serve each other? By giving individuals a greater range of choice in deciding their life careers can we at the same time ensure a more flexible labour supply which will be more responsive to future changes in manpower requirements? While aiming at the economic objective of a more rational utilisation of human resources, can we at the same time enlarge individual freedom? Might there not be other economic and social benefits which would flow from fostering more flexible patterns of working life (for instance, avoidance of "waste" in educational expenditure, and reduction of the existing sense of frustration among some groups of the population)? A first step is to question whether existing rigidities are justified.

Avoiding rigidities in life patterns

Can we any longer tolerate that, on or before the end of compulsory schooling, an adolescent should be expected to select his life occupation in the knowledge that a switch later will not be easy? Is it right that a young person who has passed a fixed entry age for a training course or an apprenticeship should be shut out from certain occupations, or that he should not be able to make up later in life for missed educational opportunities?

Can it be made easier for those who, at certain stages in their lives, want to do other things than performing regular full-time work to do so? For instance, can more alternatives to regular full-time work be offered to women with family responsibilities? Are there ways of allowing an older worker, some years before normal retirement age, to take time off while he is still fully active in order to study for some leisure pursuit which will later help him to enjoy his retirement, or perhaps in order to indulge some

long-standing ambition to travel? When a worker reaches
pensionable age, what arrangements can be made to help him
to continue to work if he wants to do so? These are only a
few examples of points in a person's life career when a more
flexible approach may be needed.

These rigidities do not exist to the full extent in
all European countries or for all categories of persons. In
fact, a good deal is being done to provide more
opportunities for individual choice and for individual
adjustment to changing manpower requirements. There is some
recognition that the normal human life need no longer
consist of a sequence of separate, self-contained periods:
(1) infancy, (2) school, (3) vocational training or higher
studies, (4) regular full-time employment, to be followed by
(5) retirement once and for all somewhere between 60 and 67
(or earlier withdrawal from the labour force in the case of
married women).

A few of the changes which have taken place may be
mentioned. Girls now realise that their working life is
likely to consist of three phases - (1) a relatively short
period of full-time employment before marriage and the
arrival of the first child, (2) temporary withdrawal from
the labour force while they care for their young children,
to be followed by (3) a substantial period of more or less
regular employment. Workers approaching retirement age find
more options open to them such as (a) to draw their
retirement benefits at the minimum age and withdraw from the
labour force, (b) to continue in full-time or part-time
employment and thereby increase their later retirement
benefits or (c) to draw their retirement benefits and
continue such full-time, part-time, intermittent or seasonal
employment as is permitted without adversely affecting these
benefits. More workers than in the past are interested in
part-time or intermittent employment and more employers are
prepared to change their employment practices to meet this
desire (in some cases this may be the only way of meeting
their labour needs); more young people seek to avoid
premature commitment to a lifelong career and look for a
variety of experience, at home or abroad, before they settle
down. Are the future effects of these trends being properly
considered? Are there ways of making use of them to solve
some of the problems observed in the previous chapter? How
are these trends likely to develop? Should positive efforts
be made to develop them further, and, if so, in what
direction?

It is perhaps time for those concerned with employment
policy to attempt to put the old fixed patterns of working
life out of their minds as the only possible patterns.
While many persons, perhaps the majority, might, even when
offered alternatives, prefer to follow the traditional
patterns, employment planners would be well advised to think
of the labour force not as a quantity pre-determined by
demographic factors but as a dynamic element, the volume and

characteristics of which can vary at any point within a
person's active years. The more opportunity a worker has
over his lifetime to shape his own destiny, the more
adaptable and productive he is likely to be. And, looking
ahead, it is useful to bear in mind that rising living
standards will, in the future, both enhance the desire for
greater freedom of control over the use of one's active
years as an important element in the "quality of life" and
increase the possibilities of meeting this desire.

Study and work

As regards general schooling, most educational theory
now favours closer contacts between school and the world of
work, particularly in any additional year of compulsory
education for the less academically able children. A short
period of work experience is also now seen as a valuable
element in vocational orientation. Concurrently, more of
those young people who enter employment directly from school
(whether as apprentices, trainees or otherwise) are required
to continue with a certain amount of general education. The
frontier between school and work is thus becoming less
sharply defined, and the transition easier.

So far so good. But it still remains the most
widespread practice for vocational training or higher
education to be a process which is entered immediately
after, or very soon after, termination of schooling. It is
still a rarity for the individual who has gone straight from
school into work to have an equal chance later in his career
of achieving the same standard of vocational training or
higher education, although this might not only be more
equitable but also offer the prospect of training or
education more directly relevant to his employment.

It has become commonplace to say that many jobs today
require more highly specialised knowledge than at any time
in the past, but that this knowledge becomes obsolete more
rapidly than ever before. From this situation, it has been
deduced that education should be "permanent", "continuous"
or "recurrent", which means spreading education over the
individual's life-span in a recurring way, that is, in
alternation with work as well as with leisure and, possibly
retirement.[1] At present, many young people are swept
straight from secondary school into full-time higher

----

[1] OECD Centre for Educational Research and Innovation:
Clarifying report on recurrent education, (Paris, 1972)
(CERI/CD(72)22); also OECD: Continuing training and
education during working life, papers prepared for an
international conference, Copenhagen, July 1970.

education before they have really identified their interests. They should be given the opportunity of a breathing space and of going to work which would allow them to have a clearer idea of the field of studies they wish to follow and to be better motivated to profit from the form of post-secondary education they ultimately choose. It is also argued that, gradually, as alternatives become more widespread and better known, this would reduce pressure for entry to full-time university education direct from secondary school, and that this would in turn help to reduce the present excessive rate of growth of expenditure on this part of the educational system.

There are some occupations for which this would perhaps not be desirable. For instance, it is said that training for the medical profession will almost always have to follow immediately on secondary education, partly because it is long, and partly because it is essential that the student's basic scientific knowledge should be fresh.[1] There are also fewer disadvantages in sequential education in this case: a firm vocational choice has already been made, the student faces the realities of his working life at a fairly early stage in his studies and the need for refresher courses later in life has already been acknowledged. But in many other occupations, it is argued that higher education, now almost exclusively given at the end of school, would be put to much better use by maturer students with some experience of work, who would have a clearer idea of what they wanted to study and of its bearing on their future working life, combined with better motivation to complete their studies.

A system of deferred higher education might provide answers to some of the problems described in Chapter III, for example, the waste involved in the continuous flow of young students to universities for such reasons as (a) they are qualified for entry, and education is almost "something for nothing", (b) going to the university is a way of delaying occupational choice and other difficult decisions, (c) to please their parents, or (d) a diploma or degree is thought to be a passport to higher income and social status.

Such a system would be more equitable in that it would give a better chance to those from less favoured social backgrounds who may only reveal their abilities and their motivation to study after having been out in the world of work. It would be fairer to those women who marry young and only have the opportunity and the urge to study when their

----

[1] Though even in this case it has been suggested in the Federal Republic of Germany that it would be better for would-be medical students who cannot immediately be accommodated in medical schools to do practical work in hospitals rather than to mark time in other faculties of the university as they do at present (see pp. 60-61).

children have reached nursery-school age or after. In countries with periods of compulsory military service, it might even offer an answer to the thorny question of postponement of service in order to complete studies.

Moreover, a system of recurrent education would also have far-reaching effects on the labour market inasmuch as it is likely to bridge the gap between education and work more effectively than is presently the case. Those pleading in favour of recurrent education stress that the alternation of schooling and work would lead to a more satisfactory adaptation of education to the needs of the labour market for qualified people and facilitate greater occupational mobility of the labour force.[1] However, the introduction of such schemes clearly means rethinking and reshaping the present educational system which could, of course, only take place gradually.

Recurrent education has recently come into the foreground in debate on future educational strategies[2]; it has not yet gone much beyond the stage of a widely discussed proposition. Certain aspects of recurrent education are already being tested here and there and it is arousing wide interest in a growing number of countries. Thus in Sweden, where high priority is given to educational equality, there are schemes to bridge the educational gap between today's young who benefit from extensive education and earlier generations, that is the majority of the population aged 15-65 who had only 6-7 years of schooling. Although recurrent education aims in the long run at incorporating both youth and adult education in one system, interim measures are being taken to expand general education for adults, affecting approximately 100,000 people in 1970-71; these measures are designed to help adults with short basic education to cope better with the changing needs of the labour market and of society.

The Open University in the United Kingdom was originally conceived to offer a second chance to adults who had missed the opportunity of entering higher education on leaving school or who, like women with young children, could not attend normal higher education institutions. Many of the Open University's innovative measures, especially its use of new educational techniques, are relevant to the concept of recurrent education. One of the original features is the modular approach to the curriculum which allows great flexibility in the combination of subjects

----

[1] Ibid., p. 59-60.

[2] The Swedish 1968 Educational Commission (U 68) launched recurrent education in 1969 as a new educational strategy distinct from the present sequential system which provides uninterrupted education between the ages of 7 and 25.

chosen by the individual student according to his needs. Students all over the country - 25,000 enrolled during the first year 1971 - are taught through radio and television, through correspondence, at local tutorial centres and at the yearly one-week residential summer schools. One of the problems, however, seems to be that in the first intake, the majority of the students were from the teaching and other professions and had already gone beyond secondary education, while manual workers were strongly under-represented.[1] The enrolment of women (27 per cent) was not higher than that for other universities, but 13 per cent of the applicants in 1972 were housewives and drop-out rates were lower for women than for men.

Similar difficulties in attracting the educationally under-privileged to further education and training schemes are experienced in several other countries. Unless legal or other provisions exist for paid leave of absence from work for education and training purposes[2], educational activities usually take place during leisure time and are in many cases on a fee-paying basis. Even in the traditional workers' educational institutions of a number of Western European countries, the people's high schools, the participation rate of manual workers has considerably decreased. And where financial help is available to improve the occupational mobility of the labour force, as for instance in the Federal Republic of Germany, the chief beneficiaries of the Employment Promotion Act of 1969 are reported to be young men, already fairly well established in their occupations who use their training for advancement. In France too, concern is voiced by the trade unions that top and middle management as well as already well-trained technical personnel are likely to benefit more from the 1971 legislation on continuous training than manual workers. There is nothing wrong in training for advancement (it may be wholly desirable from the point of view of the economy) but it is clear that if any system of recurrent education or training is intended to replace higher education given straight after schooling, then some special measures must be introduced to ensure that it gives equal opportunities to those who had inferior educational opportunities in their younger years.

Selection clearly should be based not only on certificates acquired at the end of secondary education, but much more on the record of performance at work, supplemented perhaps by tests of aptitude, interest, and some assessment of motivation. There would also be implications for

----

[1] The first teaching year of the Open University, Report of the Vice-Chancellor (Bletchley, March 1973).

[2] ILO: Paid educational leave, Report VI (1) and VI (2), International Labour Conference, 58th Session, Geneva, 1973.

secondary school curricula, which would need to have terminal elements so that the student would be qualified either to start work and continue along vocational streams, or to proceed later to higher education.

In Yugoslavia, for instance, there are already educational institutions (regional school centres) which combine secondary-level general and vocational education with the first year of higher education.[1] In these centres, both youth and adults are educated side by side and are offered "multi-stage" education, i.e. the possibility of acquiring qualifications for a particular job and of continuing studies at a higher level. Close contacts are maintained between these centres and industrial undertakings in the region.

The move away from the "job for life"

A generation or so ago, the ambition of almost all parents was to see their children settled in a job for life. The young people themselves often concurred in this parental choice because they too valued employment security, and the only way of achieving this security seemed to be by taking a life-time job. But the present generation, at least in countries north of the Alps, has grown up in a climate of full employment and the life-time job has lost much of its appeal. Types of employment which used to rely on the guarantee of a job for life to attract candidates have found themselves falling short of applicants: the police, postal services, and the railways provide examples. Even in those countries which have experienced higher unemployment since 1967, the guarantee of a job for life has not regained its appeal. Young people are more interested in other characteristics of a job such as the status which it confers on them among their contemporaries, the extent of job satisfaction which it offers, the immediate earnings, or the prospects of rapid advancement. It is perhaps symptomatic that publicity designed to attract young applicants for instance to the police no longer stresses the job security aspects but other features such as the human and social interest of the work, the variety of experience which it offers, or the chance to exercise individual responsibility.

In the Socialist countries the problem may not arise in the same form. But the high labour turnover rates in the younger age groups suggest that there is some restlessness and a desire to experiment with different types of employment.

----

[1] B. Sefer: Local and regional centres for recurrent education: Yugoslav experience and orientation, OECD, Centre for Educational Research and Innovation (Paris, March 1973), CERI/RE/73.05.

Many sociological explanations are offered for this change of attitude by youth. It is sometimes suggested that the world is changing so fast that the young cannot envisage, or prefer not to think, what it will be like in 20 or 30 years' time and how they will fit in to it. There is a certain pessimism about the future of society as a whole, while there is at the same time considerable optimism among individuals about their own ability to adjust to changes. This means that time horizons are shorter than in the past, and that young workers expect, even hope, to change their employer, their industry or their occupation every so many years; in fact, for many the prospect of doing the same kind of work under similar conditions for the rest of their working lives is repellent. The younger generation brought up with a broader range of knowledge and more open outlook regard such a pattern of working life as one of the constraints of modern industrial and commercial society from which they want to break loose.

In the private sector of industry and commerce in Western Europe, this coincides to some extent with shorter time horizons on the part of employers, who are now prepared to accept a higher rate of turnover than in the past.

In certain spheres of work where life-long employment is traditional - the civil service and university teaching for instance - there is new appreciation that positive gains can be derived from occupational mobility. The move of highly-qualified people between public administration, industry, research and teaching not only makes for cross-fertilisation of ideas, but gives the persons concerned a wider understanding of the problems with which they are required to deal.

In all cross-movements of this kind, problems of transferability of pension may arise, and importance needs to be attached to ensuring that they do not over-inhibit desirable occupational mobility.

The few longitudinal studies that have been made of samples of the labour force in Western European countries[1] seem to show that in practice workers (and not only young workers) make many more, and more fundamental, changes of employment than has usually been assumed. Many cases are found in which workers do not remain in the occupation for which they have been trained; in other cases, workers who have had no formal training are found to be performing in an occupation just as successfully as those who have had formal training for it. Employment planners are realising that the picture is not neat and tidy, and that easy assumptions

----

[1] For instance, those carried out by the Employment and Occupational Research Institute of the Federal German Employment Institution covering the employment of a sample of male workers in 1955, 1965 and 1970.

about training a given number of workers to fill a foreseen
number of vacancies cannot be made.

This higher volume of mobility than is usually allowed
for has both advantages and disadvantages for the economy.
It should mean greater adaptability of the labour force to
the needs of structural change. But much of it is
fortuitous and haphazard, serves little economic purpose,
and involves waste of past training and low productivity at
the start of a new job. The aim of policy needs to be to
see that as much as possible of this mobility is in the
right direction. One approach is to provide retraining
courses in shortage occupations for those without
employment, or threatened with loss of employment, and to
see that the public knows about them and makes use of them.[1]

In theory, it would be desirable for every person of
any age contemplating a job change to seek occupational
guidance, but no European country (or country in any part of
the world for that matter) can be said to have a guidance
service which the majority of job changers would
automatically think of consulting on these occasions. At
present, whether or not a job change serves the cause of
adaptation to structural change and the more efficient use
of manpower is largely a matter of the quality of the
advertising and selection methods used by the employers or
of pure chance.

In the Socialist countries, the view is more generally
taken that labour turnover is wasteful and that it tends to
frustrate rational manpower planning; mobility, it is felt,
should rather be within the same undertaking or at least the
same industry. The _juste milieu_ between excessive labour
turnover and desirable labour mobility is not easy to find.

A new phenomenon in the more affluent of the Western
European countries is the growing number of young people who
have left the world of education without yet having settled
in the world of work. Many are not unemployed in the usual
sense of the term and would not regard themselves as such.
They may be continuing with desultory study, supplemented by
occasional work just sufficient to bring in enough money for
them to continue to live at the low standard to which they
have been accustomed as students. They may remain as
hangers-on around a university; they may be travelling
cheaply abroad to see societies different from their own;
they may be searching for some alternative way of living to
the consumer society.

----

[1] Some success along these lines has been achieved in
Sweden, where repeated discussion of labour market problems
in the mass media has led to better understanding by the
general public of the direction in which employment
opportunities lie, and where the idea of adults taking
labour market training courses when they are faced with the
need to change their occupation has taken root.

The number is difficult to assess, chiefly because those concerned seek the minimum contact with the authorities. But an interesting analysis has been made in France[1] which classified their activities into four types: (a) prolonged post-educational activities such as coaching schoolchildren, baby sitting, working in holiday camps, helping in opinion polls, acting as hospital auxiliaries; (b) casual labouring bearing no relation to their education such as working as storemen, packers, car washers or drivers; (c) self-employment chosen for its independence, such as working on fairgrounds, acting as cinema extras, performing in pop groups, making and selling handicraft jewellery; and (d) para-delinquent or pre-delinquent activities.

How far should the employment authorities be concerned with this section of the population? Should its members be left alone (as most of them would wish)? Should they be left to develop their own parallel labour market systems[2], or should the authorities try to meet them half-way and try to help them make better use of their potential? A source of casual workers concerned more with the type of the work than with its monetary rewards may be a useful addition to the labour force (for instance in auxiliary hospital work). Young travellers already do useful seasonal work in harvesting if they are provided with a social environment which appeals to them. The desire for foreign travel too can be a positive factor; the need for improved linguistic knowledge has been better met as a result of girls working au pair in a foreign country, and of secretaries travelling round the world on working holidays; there is often talk of the value of reviving the old European tradition of Wanderjahre in different occupations as a way of enhancing individual maturity, occupational standards and international comprehension.

Sooner or later, most of this group are likely to have to face the need to accept some more regular work bringing in a more regular income and making better use of their education and training. Should more thought be given to ways in which they can be helped to re-enter the normal labour market?

----

[1] Jean Rousselet: "Les activités 'marginales' des jeunes", in Centre d'Etudes de l'Emploi: Bulletin d'information, No. 6, November 1972.

[2] For instance in the United Kingdom, the press has reported the existence of (1) an organisation called "Uncareers" which publishes a guide to alternative employment and (2) young people's co-operatives supplying temporary workers in a wide range of occupations.

Special arrangements for women workers

Changes in women's working life patterns

The group whose working life patterns changed most visibly in the 1960s was that of women with family responsibilities. The changes noted in a report for the 48th Session of the International Labour Conference in 1964[1] have continued.

Patterns of the years of employment and years of other duties vary greatly between communities, depending, for instance, on the level of demand for labour, the proportion of the female labour force engaged in agriculture or housework, educational standards, social traditions and the extent of child-care facilities. By way of example, the patterns emerging from two studies undertaken, one in the Federal Republic of Germany, and the other in the United Kingdom, may be summarised, though they are not necessarily representative of the position in other countries or groups.

The former survey[2] distinguishes six phases. First, entry into work between the ages of 14 and 20, with a tendency for the age of entry to become higher as girls tend to stay at school longer, and for the spell of work to become shorter because of a tendency to marry earlier. In the United Kingdom[3], this first phase, once seven years, has fallen on average to less than five. Women then leave work, usually because of childbirth and in order to look after their children and household; they may also leave their job, though not necessarily give up work, through change of abode on getting married. The study in the Federal Republic of Germany places this interval at about 8 years, usually between the ages of 20 and 37 1/2, whereas the British report refers to a gap of 12 to 15 years. The tendency is for this period to become shorter, as the trend is towards having fewer children and those fairly closed spaced. The third phase, re-entry into work, is more variable in its effect. In some cases, women then carry on in employment

----

[1] ILO: Women workers in a changing world, International Labour Conference, 48th Session, Geneva, 1964.

[2] Hans Kohler and Lutz Reyher: "Erwerbsttätigkeitsphasen der Frauen" in Mitteilungen aus der Arbeitsmarkt- und Berufsforschung, 1970, No. 3, pp. 286-297 (reprint available) (Stuttgart, Berlin, Cologne and Mainz, Verlag W. Kohlhammer, 1970).

[3] Central Training Council: The training of women returning to office work after a break and other adults entering this field of work for the first time. A report by the Commercial and Clerical Training Committee (London, 1970) (mimeographed).

until retirement age, so that, in the United Kingdom, it is estimated that there is likely to be another 20 or 25 years of useful employment, making with the initial spell a total of about 30 years. In the Federal Republic of Germany, however, a further phase is noted, occurring around 47 1/2 to 52 1/2 years of age, when more women leave work than return to it. After about 52 1/2 years of age, the position is reversed, but the difference is relatively slight. At the end of the span of working life, there is in the Federal Republic of Germany a substantial increase in the number of those over 65 at work.

In the Socialist countries, this division into phases is generally less marked, with the interval for child bearing and child rearing being on the whole shorter. The service to society performed by mothers who stay at home to care for their young children is recognised by appropriate social security benefits, but it is normally taken for granted that they will want to resume their employment as soon as possible. There are generous provisions for the retention of employment and social security rights during their absence. For instance, in Poland unpaid leave of up to three years for each childbirth is authorised (in certain circumstances this can be extended to six years); this carries the right to reinstatement in the job previously vacated. In practice, only a minority exercise their right to return to precisely the same employment, and few wait for the full three years. In Czechoslovakia, mothers retain the right to reinstatement in their old job or an equivalent one up to two years after confinement, but in practice, two-thirds of them return to their employment within a year. In Hungary, similar reinstatement rights exist and the trade unions make a great point of seeing that they are implemented, but there is a special demographic situation: the Government wishes to raise the present low birth rate, particularly from the mid-1970s to 1985 when the number of women of child-bearing age will be low. It has found that payment to the mother of a child-care allowance up to the end of the third year following the birth of a child has a favourable effect on the birth rate; this incentive to stay at home will therefore be continued for the time being.

Training for return to employment

The Western European countries, in which, as has been seen, the period of absence from employment is normally longer than in Eastern Europe, have found that women returning to the labour force are often in need of training of one kind or another, whether it is in their old occupation to bring them up to date with changed processes introduced during their absence or in an entirely new occupation.[1] Absence of education and training possibilities

----

[1] B.N. Seear: Re-entry of women to the labour market after an interruption in employment (OECD, Paris), 1971.

for women, particularly in their thirties and forties, leave most of them with no choice other than to take up unskilled and often lower paid jobs. Here again, recurrent education could give a second opportunity to women who interrupted their studies or careers to raise a family and who, for one reason or another, wish to re-enter employment.[1] Recurrent education would make it possible for women not only to raise their general educational standard but through training or retraining to improve their chances in the labour market and thus be on a more equal footing with men than is at present the case. In several countries such as France, Federal Republic of Germany and Sweden, special encouragement is given to women to re-enter the labour force through a variety of training opportunities.

In Eastern European countries, the need for re-entry training seems in general to be less acutely felt because of the shorter absence from work, though in Hungary a working group on population and employment planning recently observed that staying several years at home made it more difficult for women to return to work, particularly in skilled occupations, and that their earnings dropped behind those of other workers; it suggested that the problem would be alleviated if more effective measures were taken at least to maintain the skills of women staying at home.[2]

Child-care facilities

In the Socialist countries, it is general policy that crèches and kindergartens should be provided so that mothers of young children can exercise their right to work if they so wish. For several decades this has been, and remains, the policy in the USSR, where it is held that the provision of well-equipped pre-school institutions, staffed by professionally trained teachers, not only relieves the mother of anxiety for her children during working hours and allows her to lead a fuller life but is positively beneficial for the children concerned. For this reason, an alternative proposal some years' ago to give child-care allowances to mothers of children under 3 so that they could look after them at home was rejected. There is variation in the extent of provision in different Socialist countries and some voices are heard arguing that in many cases it may make better sense to pay a mother to look after her own young children than to employ other women to do so. The tightness of the labour market is a factor in the variations. In the

----

[1] Gisela Schade: Recurrent education for women, Centre for Educational Research and Innovation, (Paris, 1973), CERI/RE/73.02.

[2] Reported by P. Iván and Zs. Mausecz in: "Population and employment policy: Forecast for 1985", Acta Oeconomica, (Budapest), Vol. 9(1), 1972,

German Democratic Republic, it was reported in 1971 that 69 per cent of all children between 2 and 6 were in kindergartens and 28 per cent in crèches, while an inquiry in Poland in 1970 covering a sample of women from 21 to 47 years of age living in towns found that only 12 per cent had the opportunity to place their small children (up to 3 years' old) in a crèche and 35 per cent to place their children between 3 and 6 years in a kindergarten. Other measures to facilitate the employment of women with young children include provisions for leave on full pay to look after sick children (for instance up to 60 days per year in Poland and up to 13 weeks a year in the German Democratic Republic in the special case of mothers in fatherless families).

The importance of leave for family emergencies and child-care facilities in achieving employment equality for women was also emphasised in two recent reports in the United Kingdom, one relating to the employment of women in the civil service (which has since been accepted as a basis for government policy) and one by a House of Commons committee concerned with the position of women over the whole employment field. These were however only items among several recommendations covering also part-time work, flexible hours, retraining after absence and special arrangements when a husband's employment mobility requires that the family should move to another area. In both cases, the recommendations were made in relation to implementing the principle of equality of the sexes rather than to their effects on the labour force.

A further problem which was already touched on in the discussions on the employment of women at the time of the 48th Session of the International Labour Conference is that any concessions to women workers which impose heavy charges on the employer run the danger of being counterproductive. It is still occasionally reported for instance that some undertakings in Socialist countries, because of these charges, prefer not to employ women between 25 and 45 if any other source of labour is available.

Flexible hours and part-time work

However, certain measures, like the arrangement of flexible hours, have been shown not to result in any very heavy charges on the employer. In fact, recent experience in some Western European countries suggests that flexible hours may bring a bonus in the form of reduced tension at the workplace and consequently lower rates of labour turnover. This is not the place to go into the subject in detail[1], but it may be remarked here that this is a field where it is proving possible to give workers more freedom to

---

[1] See the Report of the Director-General, pp. 43-44.

determine their own working lives in line with the suggestion made at the beginning of this chapter.

Part-time employment is increasingly resorted to as a way of meeting the employment problems of women with family responsibilities. In some Western European countries, employers badly in need of labour are now ready to arrange a great variety of unusual hours or special shifts to suit the needs of different categories of women which they would at one time have considered quite impracticable.

In a report on the application of the employment policy instruments, the Government of the USSR mentioned that one of the current aims of its policy was to facilitate the employment of those who could not work a full day. In the German Democratic Republic, of the married women between 18 and 60 in gainful employment in 1970, half worked part-time (one-third of these working less than 22 hours a week). It is not the intention here to raise the whole complex subject of part-time work but merely to indicate that it holds a significant place among the means of giving more flexibility to the labour force.

Intermittent employment

Another way in which women with family responsibilities contribute to the labour force is in temporary employment, for instance by being available on call to replace workers absent on sickness or on holiday, or to stop temporary gaps in personnel, particularly in offices, hospitals and shops. The potential for organisation of this section of the labour market was first appreciated in North America by private agencies; private temporary work agencies then spread to those Western European countries where their activities were not held to be illegal[1] and their commercial success suggests that they are meeting a need. In the Scandinavian countries and the Federal Republic of Germany, public services have made efforts to meet this need, either in place of or in competition with the private agencies, but this seems to be an area in which the private sector has, at least hitherto, been more successful. Several governments have limited their intervention to a policy of regulating these agencies. From the point of view of drawing women workers into the labour market, the contribution of the agencies seems to be positive, but governments are keeping their operations under review to see that abuses do not arise.

----

[1] For certain legal aspects which are not the concern of this report, see N. Valticos: "Temporary work agencies and international labour standards", _International Labour Review_ (Geneva, ILO), January 1973 and G.M.J. Veldkamp and M.J.E.H. Raetsen: "Temporary work agencies and Western European social legislation", ibid., February 1973.

Nothing comparable exists in the Socialist countries, partly because employment fluctuates less and because undertakings draw on their own labour reserve to meet any fluctuations that arise. However, undertakings in the USSR are allocated a small part of the wage fund which is not committed to their regular work force and which is available for emergencies which are sometimes met for instance by the temporary employment of their retired personnel.

Special arrangements for the third age

The term "third age" is not precise. If we want to use demographic statistics we have arbitrarily to situate this as beginning at 65, although for analysis of the employment problems of older persons this is not an entirely satisfactory limit to take. Some types of work are clearly too arduous to expect workers to remain in them up to that age and some workers do not remain fit enough right up to that age to be regarded as full members of the labour force. Conversely, some types of work can be done just as well by people of 65 or over, and some workers of this age are both fit and anxious to carry on with their usual employment and to be treated on an equal plane with younger workers. Society's attitude too varies. The normal retirement age (which can be taken as society's recognition of the age by which it is thought that a worker has made an adequate contribution to the economy and has earned a rest) ranges from 60 (or lower in the case of women, or of men who have worked in certain industries) up to 67.

Nevertheless, 65 is the most convenient starting point to take. If we take this as the beginning of the third age, the first face to note is that persons of 65 and over are progressively coming to form a larger proportion of the total population of European countries.

The aging of the European population

An interesting study of the aging of the population of Europe (excluding USSR) and its social and economic consequences, was presented at the Council of Europe Second European Population Conference in 1971.[1] Table 8 in the Appendix to this report draws on data from that study and

----

[1] H. Damas and L. Neundörfer: Rapport sur les aspects démographiques du vieillissement de la population en Europe et ses conséquences sociales et economiques (with summary in English) Council of Europe, Second European Population Conference, Strasbourg, 31 August-7 September 1971. (doc. CDE(71)T.I.)

shows the growing share of persons 65 and over in the total
population of 29 European countries from 1950 to 1960 and
again to 1968 (approximate dates); there is a particularly
appreciable increase in the older female group. The study
points out that this aging of the population has hitherto
been mainly caused by changes in reproductive behaviour and
not by an increase in the percentage of persons reaching old
age. Another interesting aspect which it brings out is
that, except for 4 out of the 581 regions analysed, older
persons still represent numerically less of a "burden" on
the working population than the young (those below 15 years
of age).

Most of the implications of this aging of the
population lie in fields outside the concern of this report,
such as the provision of medical services, income
maintenance, housing and social services for those 65 years'
old or over. But the increase in their numbers also has
implications for manpower policy. If some of them can be
helped to remain in the labour force this alleviates their
other problems. The physiological and psychological need to
work does not cease abruptly at 65 or at any other arbitrary
age and persons should be given the opportunity to meet this
need; and if appropriate adjustments can be made, those of
the third age can be a useful marginal source of manpower.

Although the USSR is not included in table 8, the same
problem exists there, where the view is taken that the
psychological and physiological needs of older persons
cannot be met by measures which segregate them from other
age groups; in cases where retention in wage-paid
employment is not possible or is not desired, efforts are
made to keep older people in close contact with the rest of
the community through voluntary work, for instance in
connection with the leisure activities of youth or
improvement of the environment.

To speak of persons of the third age as a marginal
source of manpower does not mean that there should be any
pressure on them to stay in or re-enter the labour force
against their inclination; they have earned the right to
retire and this is inviolable. It implies that measures
should be taken to see that they are not arbitrarily
excluded from employment; to provide facilities and
incentives for those who want to work and, in doing so, to
be prepared to envisage the design of suitable work for them
or to arrange special working conditions or hours.

Arbitrary retirement ages

In referring to retirement ages, one is sometimes
talking about two different things: (1) the age at which
retirement pension becomes payable, and (2) the age at which
the worker chooses, or is required by his employer, to stop
regular work. In practice the two often coincide, but there

is no valid reason why they should always do so. A flexible
retirement policy involves making each of these ages less
rigid and at the same time seeing that age (1) does not have
a rigid determining influence on age (2).[1]

Some social security schemes have a range of ages
within which the insured person can choose the moment to
retire and start receiving his pension: the value of the
latter rises as retirement is deferred, partly because
account is taken of the additional contributions paid, and
partly because of actuarial estimations of the number of
years over which the pension is likely to be paid. This
provides some scope for individual choice, but often the
choice is determined for the individual by the contractual
or customary age at which the employer terminates employment
of his workers, since in few occupations is a worker over
60, once discharged, able easily to find steady employment
with a fresh employer. However, it does provide freedom for
the employer and the worker mutually to adjust the date of
retirement according to individual wishes and the current
labour supply and demand situation.

In exceptional cases, where it is desired to reduce
the work force in a particular industry, the effective
pensionable age may be lowered. The use of this device as
a means of adjustment to structural change is described in
Report III.

Flexible pensionable ages are less often found in
supplementary occupational pension schemes or those of
undertakings. In the latter, the age is normally related
directly to the internal manpower planning of the
undertaking and the worker is expected to retire at about
the date when he becomes eligible for pension. There is the
dilemma that any prolongation of his employment would block
the promotion avenues for younger personnel and disrupt the
normal rhythm of recruitment and replacement. In some
fields of employment an attempt to meet this dilemma is made
by providing that, though workers are required to leave
their jobs on reaching pensionable age, they may continue to
be employed in a junior post, or in temporary jobs.

In certain social security systems there is a broader
range of choice of retirement age for the insured person
than for the employer. For instance in Romania, male
workers can choose to retire at 60, but undertakings cannot
choose to terminate the employment of these workers until

----

[1] A general discussion of these ideas and a description
of the situation in this respect in France, Federal Republic
of Germany, and the United Kingdom is contained in OECD:
Flexibility of retirement age (Paris, 1970); see also OECD:
Adaptation and employment of special groups of manpower.
Conclusions of the Manpower and Social Affairs Committee on
Older Workers.

they are 62 years' old (in agriculture the respective ages
are 5 years' later).

In the Socialist countries generally, the situation is
affected by the low pensionable age (as a rule, 60 for men,
55 for women). If the pensionable age were being fixed de
novo today, it is probable that it would be higher, having
regard to the present age-distribution of the labour force,
the lighter nature of most employment, and the improved
health of workers in their late fifties and early sixties.
However, the low pensionable age is looked upon as a
historically significant social achievement which cannot be
withdrawn, although it may have lost much of its original
raison d'être. Policy is therefore directed towards making
it easier for those who have reached pensionable age to stay
on at work.

In all countries, pension systems should be such as to
encourage rational labour market behaviour by older workers
and their employers.

Employment of pensioners

Pensioners who stay at work continue to make a
valuable contribution to the labour force in many European
countries. To take a striking example, in the German
Democratic Republic (where the labour force has been
stagnant and the proportion of older women in the population
very high), over 8 per cent of the female labour force is
constituted by pensioners.

Practices differ as to the possibility of drawing both
wage and pension in full. For instance in France, the
Federal Republic of Germany, Netherlands, Norway and Sweden
(among others), a worker is not required to retire in order
to receive pension; in Spain, a worker is obliged to retire
to quality for his pension; in Portugal, between the ages
of 65 and 70, retirement from insured employment is required
to be eligible for a pension, but this is not necessary from
age 70; in the United Kingdom there is an earnings test for
men from 65 to 70 and for women from 60 to 65. Against the
former practice it is argued that the pensioner is either
enjoying a much higher income than non-pensioners (which is
regarded by younger people as unfair) or else is accepting
a low wage (which tends to retard the raising of wage
levels). Against the latter practice it is argued that the
pensioner deliberately limits his activity so that his
earnings do not affect his pension. It is difficult to say
in general which system most satisfactorily combines maximum
choice by the individual with the best interests of the
labour market.

In the USSR, entitlement to pension is not contingent
on cessation of work and a worker cannot be discharged
because he becomes entitled to a pension (though in some

fields he may have to pass a medical examination). The
worker can ask to be transferred to part-time work (though
it is reported that not all workers are yet aware of the
right given them in this respect by recent legislation, and
that not all managers of enterprises are happy about the
complications which this makes for them). At the beginning
of the 1960s, there was little financial incentive for
pensioners to continue at work as they could draw only a
small part of the pension; this was changed and in the last
ten years the proportion of pensioners staying at work has
doubled (in the RSFSR, the proportion in 1972 was from 30
per cent to 34 per cent of those between 60 and 65 and 22
per cent of pensioners of all ages). For selected shortage
categories of workers (such as medical and paramedical
personnel and teachers) an experiment is being carried out
in the RSFSR whereby wage and pension can both be drawn in
full up to a maximum of 300 roubles a month (a sum which has
to be seen in relation to the average wage of 130 to 135
roubles a month).

In other Socialist countries also, a number of very
flexible arrangements exist which are designed as incentives
to encourage retention in the labour force of those
particular pensioners who are most needed without giving
excessive encouragement to others. For instance, in Poland
the amount which pensioners can earn without it affecting
their pension is fixed higher in some occupations than in
others, and the long-term plan envisages increasing this
flexibility. In Czechoslovakia, workers of retirement age
wishing to go on working have three options (a) to defer
their pension till a later date, when it will be paid at a
higher rate, (b) to draw pension plus wage up to a specific
ceiling, or (c) to draw pension at full rates and perform
temporary or seasonal work not exceeding 120 days per year
(180 in specific cases). In Romania, pensioners can work
four months a year without it affecting their pensions; if
they work a full year they have the option of taking full
pension plus half-wage, or half-pension plus full wage; and
there are special exceptions in some industries short of
skilled manpower in which the pensioner can draw both in
full.

A variety of solutions have thus been adopted in
different European countries. Some rules still stem from
times of labour surplus when it may have been appropriate to
discourage pensioners from continuing to work; others have
been adapted to the new circumstances.

Transition from work to retirement

The Prime Minister of France, in presenting his
Government's programme to the National Assembly in April
1973, referred to persons between the ages of 60 and 65 and
dwelt on the advantages of arrangements which provide a
transition from full activity to complete withdrawal from

employment; his Government approved the principle of experiments along these lines.[1]

Flexible pension arrangements are one aspect of this transition; another is that of the gradual phasing out of work. A number of major companies in the United Kingdom for instance run pre-retirement courses for their personnel, and gerontologists are investigating the potential effect of progressively shorter working hours and progressively longer holidays in easing the transition. In the USSR too, experiments are being made in some regions with pre-retirement advice for older workers in which gerontological group consultations are given by retired doctors. A list of recommended suitable jobs for pensioners has been compiled.

One company in France has introduced a voluntary phasing-out system under which its workers can ask to have their working week reduced as follows:

Age	Reduction
60-62	1 day
62-63	1 1/2 days
63-64	2 days
64-65	2 1/2 days

There is partial compensation for loss of earnings as follows:

Length of Service	Compensation
30 years	80 per cent
25 years	70 per cent
20 years	60 per cent
15 years	50 per cent

The age of 60 to 65 may be rather late to attempt to "re-process" people for the type of employment that is likely to be open to them if they choose to go on working. It is not doing a service to older workers to pretend that they have the same working capacities as younger workers; aging affects people differently, but there is often a deterioration of sight or hearing, speed of reaction, memory and time perception. This may be offset by other qualities such as greater stability, greater carefulness in regard to detail, better judgment based on longer experience and continuity with a period when higher standards of craftsmanship were insisted on.

It has been observed that workers who lose their jobs after 50 have difficulty both in finding new jobs in their
----

[1] See also Consultative Assembly of the Council of Europe: Recommendation 695(1973) on the preparation for retirement.

old occupation and in adapting to radically different
occupations. In most countries there is no longer a formal
age limit on entry to re-training courses, but relatively
few 50-year olds apply and there are still prejudices to
overcome in relation to the trainability and subsequent
employment of retrained older workers. Recent experience
shows that, with the use of the right approach and specially
adapted training procedures, considerable success can in
fact be achieved in retraining older workers; this success
needs to be made better known both to the older workers
themselves and their potential employers.

An easier solution exists when older workers are
retained by their employers and work is re-designed or
workers are re-allocated so that not so great a demand is
placed on the capacities which they are losing and more use
is made of those in which they keep up with, or even excel,
their younger colleagues. It is asking a lot of managements
to re-design work or to re-allocate workers in this way, but
the effort would seem justified. If a worker can, before
the age of 60, be transferred to a job more in keeping with
his capacities, he is more likely to want to stay on as a
willing and useful contributor to the labour force.

One way of encouraging an effective adaptation to the
third age might be to grant extended leave to a worker at
some time in his fifties when he is ready for, or in need
of, a substantial change. This could be in the form of an
"advance" of his retirement pension to be made up by work
later. The leave could be spent in re-training, in some
form of education or intellectual exercise which the person
has not had time for in his working life, in cultivation of
a hobby which will keep him active in his retirement,
perhaps in preparation for some kind of voluntary social
work, or even in travel serving no other purpose than
leisure.

Other possibilities of greater flexibility in working life

The last suggestion is only one of the many bold and
imaginative proposals pioneered by the Manpower and Social
Affairs Directorate of OECD as possible ways of reducing
present-day alienation from work and the lack of
adaptability of the labour force.[1] For instance, it is
asked, do not the considerations which inspire North
American universities to give their teaching staff
sabbatical leave and Australian governments to give their
public servants long-service leave, apply to other persons?
----

[1] For a summary, see Gösta Rehn: "For greater
flexibility of working life", OECD Observer, February 1973.

The principles of flexi-time, or working hours "à la carte", retirement "à la carte", and now education or training "à la carte" are gaining acceptance. Is it utopian to think that one day the principle of working life "à la carte" will gain acceptance? The authors of the proposals point out that it would already be technically feasible for every inhabitant of a country to have computer-recorded drawing rights for time off with pay for education, training or leisure; and that it would be possible, while still giving individuals freedom to choose when and how they draw on these credits, to influence their choice, for instance by offering bargains in reduced expenditure of credits for those who undertake retraining during a period of recession.

At first sight, these ideas may appear somewhat revolutionary, but the echo which they are now meeting shows that they touch on a deeply felt need. They deserve the most careful examination, opening up as they do simultaneous prospects of a more flexible labour market and a more evenly spread distribution of the improvements in the quality of life which it should be possible to derive from future economic growth.

CHAPTER III

THE EXPANSION OF HIGHER EDUCATION AND
THE LABOUR MARKET

In most European countries, higher education has
undergone a very rapid expansion during the last decade.
Student enrolment in higher educational institutions has
doubled and even tripled in some countries. For most of the
1960s employment opportunities for graduates from the higher
educational system kept pace with the expansion of educational opportunities. However, during the last few years
this substantial growth of higher education has been
accompanied by increasing difficulties in finding suitable
employment by graduates in a variety of subjects. Although
this phenomenon varies in extent in the different parts of
Europe, its general features are imbalances between the
supply and the demand for many categories of highly
qualified manpower. These imbalances reveal themselves in
extended periods of job-seeking, lower growth rates of
salaries, employment below the level of qualifications and
even open unemployment. The outlook for the future
employment of graduates has become an issue of growing
concern in a number of countries, in particular in those
where educational expansion has been very rapid and not
restrained by explicit labour market considerations. The
concern is all the greater since some projections indicate
that imbalances of this kind may persist for some time to
come.

However, before proposing any steps which might be
taken to meet this situation, before even suggesting
possible explanations of the difficulties, it is helpful to
examine the experience of several European countries, with
both market and socialist economies, in order to see whether
any common patterns emerge. Data are, of course, often not
strictly comparable and the perception of the problem varies
from country to country. Even so, the least that can be
said is that certain broad tendencies are strongly
suggested.

Symptoms of the problem

In so far as their perception of education and labour
market interactions is concerned, there appear to be three
groups of countries in Europe:

(i)   those which openly recognise that they have a
        graduate employment problem here and now;

(ii)   those which have no immediate problem but are
        disturbed by current trends in the number of
        qualified young people coming on to the labour
        market in relation to the foreseeable employment
        demand for them; and

(iii)   those countries where there is no evidence of a
        graduate employment problem.

    A   number of European countries including Italy,
Sweden, the United Kingdom, Netherlands and to some extent
France, to mention but a few, are seriously concerned about
current graduate employment problems. The next few pages
will devote considerable attention to the Italian and the
Swedish situations: the former because, though Italy has
fewer of its young people than some other countries in
higher education, the symptoms of education/labour force
maladjustment are acute, and a detailed examination of the
situation, therefore, gives some clues as to what to look
for in countries where the problem is more embryonic and
because, in an area in which relevant statistics are scarce,
the Italian data, although far from complete, are suggestive
of the sort of evidence that might be collected in other
countries where there is concern about the employment
problems of graduates and other educated manpower;   the
latter because Sweden has analysed its maladjustment more
thoroughly than some other countries, has reacted to it and
has gone further than others in proposing what changes
should be made.   Two non-European countries, the United
States and Canada, are also known to be seriously concerned;
their experience is of interest because their economies have
often been taken as being somewhat further along the road of
economic development on which Europe is travelling.[1]

The_Italian_situation

    In Italy, between 1961 and 1969, the number of
graduates and secondary school leavers increased much more
rapidly than the adult population as a whole. The net
result of these movements is that the proportion of the
total population who are graduates rose from 1.8 per cent in
1961 to 2.1 per cent in 1969 and of secondary school diploma
holders from 4.5 per cent to 7.0 per cent. These
proportions are small inasmuch as Italy's 1969 figure was
still below the 1961 figure for most European countries.
Therefore, if there is a graduate employment problem, it
clearly cannot be because Italy has by international
standards a high proportion of university graduates.
----

    [1] No consideration has, however, been given in this
report to the widespread educated unemployment in many parts
of the developing world which the World Employment Programme
has shown to be a disquieting feature of the economic and
social development of these countries.

However, the new graduates are not spread evenly over the
whole adult population. New graduates show an annual
increase of nearly 10 per cent. In other words, in order to
absorb them, employers need each year to recruit 10 per cent
more graduates than in the previous year. As a result,
there are wide differences between the different age groups
in the proportion of adults with high educational qualifications. For example, in 1969 3.1 per cent of the age group
35-44 had degrees compared with 1.6 per cent of the age
group 55-64. This kind of imbalance can lead to many social
tensions. For example, older managers in senior positions
may feel threatened by the better qualified younger people
and this may lead to a subconscious desire to limit their
recruitment. Conversely, the young graduates may feel that
their promotion is blocked by less well qualified older men
and may therefore complain that they are not being offered
the career chances to which their qualifications entitle
them or that employers are not making the best use of their
qualifications. In fact, according to a recent study[1], only
just over 40 per cent of all graduates considered their
degree relevant to the job they were doing. Outside the
area of education, research and the professions, only about
30 per cent of new graduates found their degree relevant to
the jobs they were doing.

Table 10.   Italy: Occupational distribution of
new graduates by sex, 1968
(percentages)

		Males	Females
Education: (i) Universities*		9.2	7.2
(ii) Schools		22.7	77.9
Research		2.8	1.0
Other public sector		18.7	4.7
(Total public sector)		(53.4)	(90.8)
Professions		17.8	5.6
Private industry and other		28.8	3.6
		100.0	100.0

* Includes study for higher degrees

Source: Quindicinale de note e commenti (CENSIS,
Rome), No. 162-63, May 1972.

The occupational distribution of new graduates by sex
as shown in table 10 indicates that well over half the men
and over 90 per cent of the women enter public sector
----

[1] Centro Studi Investimenti Sociali (CENSIS): Rapporto
sugli aspetti sociali ed economici della situazione
universitaria in Italia (Rome, 1971).

employment and less than 30 per cent of the men and 4 per cent of the women enter private industry. Perhaps even more striking is the information that over three-quarters of the women become teachers. This overwhelming dominance of the public sector in general and of education in particular has serious implications for the future employment opportunities for graduates. The education sector in particular is likely, purely for demographic reasons, to grow more slowly in the 1970s than in the previous decade unless changes are made in the teacher/pupil ratio which, in turn, will increase public expenditure on education; otherwise there will be a particularly damaging effect on the employment prospects for female graduates. According to the 1972 report on the social situation of the country, between 1970 and 1975, 280,000 university graduates and 750,000 secondary school leavers can be expected to enter the labour market. During the same period, the expansion of "traditional employment" for graduates will provide opportunities for 150,000 university graduates and 250,000 secondary school leavers. It will be necessary for something like 60 per cent of the new graduates to enter private industry compared with less than 30 per cent in 1968. This gives some measure of the employment difficulties facing Italian graduates during the next two or three years.

There is also evidence that the pattern of unemployment of qualified manpower differs considerably from that of general unemployment. In brief, the risk of unemployment for unskilled workers is with them throughout their working lives and may get worse as they approach retirement age and their physical abilities decline; conversely, for highly qualified manpower any unemployment is concentrated almost entirely at the point of initial entry into the labour force.

Table 11.   Italy: Percentage distribution of
labour force by employment category and
qualification 1969-1971

	1969	1970	1971
Employed			
Graduates	2.9	3.0	3.2
Secondary school leavers	7.3	8.2	8.9
Others	89.8	88.8	87.9
	100.0	100.0	100.0
In search of first job			
Graduates	4.2	5.8	6.3
Secondary school leavers	34.9	36.2	36.3
Others	60.8	58.0	57.4
	100.0	100.0	100.0
Unemployed			
Graduates	0.7	1.5	0.7
Secondary school leavers	9.7	11.8	9.6
Others	89.6	86.7	89.7
	100.0	100.0	100.0

Source: Quindicinale di note e commenti, op. cit.

In Italy the pattern of unemployment supports this
picture (table 11). Taking 1971 as an example, 3.2 per cent
of the employed population were graduates and just under 9
per cent were secondary school leavers. However, 6.3 per
cent of those in search of their first job were graduates
and 36 per cent were secondary school leavers. This means
that graduates were much more likely and secondary school
leavers very much more likely than those without educational
qualifications to be in search of their first job. Looking
at the unemployed, however, the picture is almost reversed.
Only 0.7 per cent of the unemployed were graduates and under
10 per cent were secondary school leavers. This means that
graduates were much less likely than unqualified people to
be unemployed once they had found their first job, while
secondary school leavers had about the same chances as their
unqualified counterparts. Taking the evidence as a whole,
secondary school leavers experienced very considerable
difficulty in finding their first job and had average
unemployment rates thereafter, graduates had difficulty in
finding their first job but had few unemployment problems
subsequently.

Finally, in the table, it is instructive to note the increase between 1969 and 1971 in the proportion of graduates seeking their first job: exactly 50 per cent. Meanwhile the proportions of employed, job-seeking and unemployed secondary school graduates all moved at approximately the same rates.

All this is consistent with the claim often made in Italy, and in several other countries also, that during recent years one important function of the university has been to provide a form of "parking" for the young in search of employment. The theory is that secondary school leavers and, increasingly, first degree graduates register or re-register as students while seeking their first job. This has led during the past year or two to an apparent stabilisation of the already bad employment situation for new secondary school leavers, but a sharp worsening of that for university graduates who eventually do have to leave the system.

In Italy, the number of students in university increased by over 50 per cent in the three years between 1969-1972, while during this period the population of normal university age grew by only some 3 per cent. Nearly all the expansion was due therefore to increases in the proportion of young people entering university and in the average length of study. Both these developments can be considered as an alternative to open unemployment. A rise in the entry rate was facilitated by the university reform of 1969 which opened all university departments to anybody who had successfully completed a secondary education. Although this made for more equality of higher education opportunity, unemployment of secondary school leavers was temporarily delayed to be faced later on, after graduation from university. Two questions which of course arise are why young people should want to delay their job search by entering and remaining in higher education and who pays for them while they do so.

The second is more easily answered than the first. It is estimated that about 30 per cent of Italian students now receive maintenance grants from the Government. Of the remainder, a large proportion are financed by their families in what is often called the "educational lottery", even for extended periods, in the expectation that when they do finally obtain employment it will be well paid and secure. Finally, an increasing proportion of students are able to maintain themselves by working in casual, temporary and part-time employment as waiters, garage attendants, shop assistants, hospital porters and so on; the casual nature of these occupations makes employers unwilling to take on full-time permanent workers covered by collective bargaining agreements. This phenomenon is, in fact, probably less marked in Italy than in some countries which have moved further along the road towards the consumer society such as France, Federal Republic of Germany, Sweden, the United States and Canada.

Why are students willing to do this and reduce their own standard of living below what it would otherwise be? If a student remains in university while waiting for a better job, why does he not become a full-time garage attendant and have a higher standard of living while he is waiting? There are at least two reasons why he should choose to remain registered as a student. The first is that despite the lower standard of living, there are for many people non-pecuniary benefits in being a student; there is a sense of community and, despite the student militancy of recent years (or perhaps because of it) being a student has a certain amount of glamour attached to it, together with some freedom from the conventions which operate against the rest of society. Secondly, there are undoubted sociological advantages in maintaining the status of student when applying for senior jobs. Society - and the average employer - accepts that students who are part-time shop assistants can apply for jobs as bank clerks or public administrators: it would be thought more strange for full-time shop assistants to do so even if they had university degrees.

It would seem, therefore, quite rational for young people who have the opportunity to do so to remain in university as long as they can while at the same time seeking suitable employment, all the more so as in 1969 salaries of graduates were still some three times the average earnings for the labour force as a whole. Clearly, even if there is a risk of unemployment or of long waiting periods, higher education still represents a good private investment.

According to some opinions, the public sector in many countries has in fact throughout the 1960s been absorbing and disguising what was in fact a surplus of graduates in relation to strict economic needs. For example, in a document on Employment prospects in the 1970s[1], submitted to an OECD conference, it was claimed that "a growing number of graduates turn to activities with a very low productivity, whose utility for the economy and society is not very clear. We are in fact witnessing a proliferation of institutions for research services, study, etc., whose objectives are sometimes confused and whose management is uncertain, their main interest being to afford a refuge for graduates". Although this may seem an extreme statement of the case, it is a widely held view and one that is at least partly confirmed by the high proportion of graduates in the public sector. It may well be that, if the public sector is to support more graduates than is economically warranted, a case could be made for maintaining them as students and

----

[1] OECD: Employment prospects in the 1970s, Inter-governmental Conference on the Utilisation of Highly Qualified Personnel (Venice, 25-27 October 1971), Document No. 6 (Paris, 1972), p. 37.

teachers in universities rather than in employment below their qualifications in public administration.

If there is a relative surplus of any particular type of manpower, it is to be expected that the earnings of that group will decline relatively to those of other categories unless there are institutional features of the labour market to prevent this from happening. In Italy, one of these institutional features is the system of nation-wide collective wage-bargaining which prevents earnings differentials between different categories of workers from changing as rapidly as would otherwise be the case. One constituent of earnings differentials that has been built into this nationally agreed wage-bargaining is educational qualification. This acts as a factor hindering labour market adjustments when demand and supply relationships change for different categories of labour. Thus, when there is a tendency for the supply of graduates to grow more rapidly than the demand, employers are inhibited from substituting them for less qualified workers as quickly as they otherwise might. This leads to graduates being unemployed or experiencing difficulty in securing their first job while the earnings differentials of those who do have jobs are maintained, rather than to a reduction in the average earnings of all graduates which would permit all the available supply to be employed. There is reported to be some evidence in Italy of secondary school leavers "renouncing" their educational qualifications in order to be able to secure employment at the wages of primary school leavers.

It is instructive to pause and reflect on this labour market adjustment process because it has two aspects that are not at all obvious but which are vital for an understanding of the relationship between educational expansion and the labour market.

In the first place, the salaries of those graduates who do find work remain high in relation to those of other employees. This enhances the "lottery" aspect of private investment in education. You may or may not be lucky in the draw for the best jobs, but if you are the rewards are substantial. The benefits as compared with the costs are accentuated if educational institutions are heavily subsidised and if students have ways of covering most of the cost of maintaining themselves. Thus the maintenance of graduate salaries above their market level combined with educational subsidies almost inevitably leads to a situation of over-supply.

The second result of the maintenance of salary differentials may be even more significant. If graduate salaries were to adjust completely to market forces, there are reasons to suppose that in many cases employers would prefer to substitute graduates for intrinsically less able workers at the same salaries. Unemployment would thus tend

to be concentrated even more than it is amongst the least
qualified workers. Trade unions representing unskilled
workers may, therefore, have more self-interest in
maintaining salary differentials than at first sight
appears, especially during a period of relative economic
stagnation.

Another possible effect of very flexible adjustments
in labour markets for qualified manpower might well be to
lead to violent fluctuations since the expectations of young
people would be extremely unstable and education is in
general a very long-term investment. At present, few people
receive any further education or training once they are
established in the labour market.

The Swedish situation

Sweden is not only geographically at the opposite end
of Europe from Italy, it is the richest country in Europe
whereas income per head in Italy is below the average. It
is also a country which has largely escaped from traditional
social and cultural patterns, whereas in Italy the force of
tradition is still strong. Nevertheless, Sweden shares with
Italy an increasing preoccupation with the problem of
finding suitable employment for its rapidly expanding output
of graduates.

Reforms in the education system as well as financial
aid programmes for students introduced in the early 1960s
greatly increased opportunities for higher education. As a
result, the demand for higher education grew more rapidly
than the capacity of universities to satisfy it. Some
faculties such as medicine, technology and certain branches
of science, therefore, had to apply the "numerus clausus".
Nevertheless, the enrolments in universities, particularly
in the "free" faculties (arts, social sciences and law),
were four times higher in 1968-69 than in 1960. This rapid
expansion has considerably increased the supply of manpower
with higher education. Applications for entry to
universities have, however, decreased since 1968 when
graduates began to meet serious difficulties in finding
employment; in addition to structural changes, the economic
recession reduced employment opportunities in general and
particularly for young people[1]; according to recent
official estimates there were some 8,000 unemployed
graduates though higher figures are also mentioned.
----

[1] In November 1972, Sweden had 107,000 "openly"
unemployed, out of a total labour force of 3.9 million. The
number of "hidden" unemployed was over 300,000, including
"involuntary" part-time workers, mainly women, latent job-
seekers, persons in retraining, on relief work, in sheltered
workshops, early retired, etc. In the case of persons under
25, unemployment rose from 15,000 in June 1970 to 39,000 in
June 1971.

It appears that students have reacted to this
situation in two ways. As in Italy, they are tending to
remain in university for longer periods and a higher
proportion are going on to post-graduate studies. However,
contrary to what happened in Italy, the proportion of
secondary school leavers who go to university has decreased;
the number of new entrants fell from 29,000 in 1968-69 to
only 22,000 in 1972. There appear to be four principal
reasons why the reaction of secondary school leavers to
graduate unemployment is different.

In the first place, unlike Italy, Sweden has a well
developed system of alternative institutions to
universities, mainly of a vocational nature. Enrolment in
these has not declined.

Secondly, a high proportion of students finance their
studies by means of loans[1], which have to be repaid out of
future income. This makes them much more conscious than
they might otherwise be of the subsequent earning potential
of their degree.

Thirdly, and closely related to the previous point,
the differentials between graduate salaries and those of
non-graduate workers are not nearly so wide as in Italy. In
fact, it hs been claimed that many graduate careers are now
in the "low income groups", with terminal earnings after tax
of $4,000-$5,000, which is little more than a vocationally
trained secondary school leaver can earn; in addition, the
latter enters employment five years earlier than the
university graduate and usually has incurred no debt in
pursuing his studies.

A fourth possible difference between the place of
higher education in Swedish society as compared with Italian
is that the status of students is not so high as in Italy.
This means that there is no advantage for a young person in
remaining registered as a student while seeking employment.
In fact, university graduates and secondary school leavers
are now competing for the same jobs and employers do not
necessarily consider a university graduate as the more
qualified or desirable recruit; students thus feel that
their efforts at university and their personal investment in
their own education may be wasted.

A report to the 1968 Educational Commission, known as
"U68", on the effect of educational expansion on the labour
market, points out:

In spite of rather important changes in the market
situation (a rapidly diminishing excess demand (for

----

[1] See Maureen Woodhall: Student loans: A review of
experience in Scandinavia and elsewhere (London University
Institute of Education, 1970).

graduates)) we have observed relatively small changes in wages and other "price" variables. This is a characteristic feature of markets with low price flexibility. The implication of this seems to be that the risk of unemployment is greater than the often expressed "risk of worse conditions of employment". If correct, there is an important task for the employees' and the employers' organisations to put more strength on the "price" flexibility in order to avoid an excess supply in the future.[1]

In other words, as in Italy, institutional factors in the labour market prevent salaries from adjusting rapidly to changed labour market conditions. During the recent recession there has, however, been a slowdown in wage increases which has had greater effects on newly recruited persons with higher education than on the average salaried employees. This tendency is the consequence of the rapid growth of supply and the ensuing surplus of graduates, which has occurred earlier in Sweden than in other European countries.

A number of innovating measures have been introduced in some faculties such as new combinations of subjects and courses and changes in curricula and teaching methods, particularly in the natural sciences where enrolment had sharply dropped over the last years. Some of the recently announced recommendations of the "U68" Educational Commission point in this direction by suggesting greater flexibility and diversification of university curricula and shorter study programmes.[2] Universities are to be decentralised to allow more equitable geographical distribution of higher education centres throughout the country. "U68" further proposes restricting the number of students in all subjects by fixing minimum and maximum limits for annual intake, with an increase of 2 per cent per year. However, no quotas will be set for recurrent education which will become the major means of attaining educational equality.

A number of special measures are also being taken by the National Labour Market Board to deal with employment problems of graduates. Temporary work programmes have been created in the public sector - work in archives or doing social surveys. In the university towns, "labour market weeks" are organised for students of different faculties with the co-operation of the universities, the student body, the employers and the County Labour Boards. Guidance

----

[1] Olof Rydh and Gunnar Österberg: Market_mechanisms_on the_labour_markets_for_higher_education_in_Sweden, Report to the 1968 Educational Commission (Stockholm, 1971; mimeographed).

[2] Arbetsmarknaden (Stockholm), No. 12, 9 April 1973, p. 4.

centres are helping students to enter occupational fields
which are new and untraditional for graduates. Thus,
courses of varying length have been set up to enable them to
acquire new or additional qualifications, for example, for
secretarial work, public health inspection, marketing and
sales techniques, pre-school education, etc. - that is,
fields in which staff are in short supply. It is often
suggested that the correct response of the educational
system to maladjustment is to provide more general education
so that graduates have more flexibility when entering the
labour market; what happens in fact is that courses tend to
become more specialised as students try to obtain specific
qualifications for the available jobs.

Other Western European countries

In the United Kingdom there is considerable concern
over declining employment opportunities for graduates.
Since the middle 1960s their labour market situation has
worsened relative to that of other workers. Over the last
ten years the number of graduates has almost doubled and in
1981 it is likely to be almost twice what it was in 1966.[1]
After a period of high employment expectations for qualified
manpower during which university and higher educational
institutions continued to grow, employment prospects after
graduation for many young people do not look very good. The
similar situation in the United States, which in the past
asborbed large numbers of British engineers and scientists,
has put a stop to the "brain-drain"; as a consequence, the
supply of engineers on the job market has greatly increased
and reports tell of hundreds of applications for few jobs in
industry and of many scientists over-qualified for the work
they are actually performing. At the same time, there was
a considerable decrease in demand from industry in the 1970-
71 academic year.[2] Recruitment for the civil service was
also reduced - in 1972 the third of the annual competitive
examinations was cancelled. Opportunities for careers in
the educational system, the major employer of graduates and
post-graduates have also diminished.[3]

----

[1] By 1981, the Government expects to be providing higher
education for about 22 per cent of the age group then aged
18 compared with 15 per cent in 1971 and 7 per cent in 1961.

[2] According to a report by the Confederation of British
Industry the reduced demand for graduate manpower is not
entirely due to the current state of the economy. It is
said to be also a reflection of an increasingly critical
approach on the part of employers to the use and economic
deployment of highly qualified manpower (Supplement to CBI
Education and Training Bulletin, February 1972).

[3] One segment of the labour market for highly qualified
manpower that is particularly affected by fluctuations is
(Footnote continued on next page)

Even a few years ago, when it was already known that earlier forecasts of population growth, the consequences of educational expansion and future manpower needs had been off the mark, this situation was hardly expected to rise. In addition, earnings of qualified manpower have risen more slowly than earnings of the labour force as a whole in recent years.[1] On the other hand, the salaries of educated people remain on the average considerably higher than those of average workers. In the mid-1960s a new graduate, even at the start of his career, could hope to be earning as much as the average earnings of unqualified workers at the peak of their career.[2] The differential is not nearly as great as in Italy, but it does show why higher education continues to be a very attractive proposition to young people, especially when it is provided virtually free of all costs as it is in the United Kingdom.

It has been estimated that if current trends continue, a surplus of graduates of about 10 per cent of the annual output could be expected by 1980 if they enter only the same type of jobs as they do at present. For women, who have increasingly made use of opportunities for higher education, the situation may eventually be even more serious. Over one-third of all female graduates are by 1980 likely to be unable to find work, even in sectors traditionally employing them, on a labour market which can no longer absorb all the male graduates. For the most part this means, of course, teaching; the surplus results directly from the expected ending of the teacher shortage in the mid-seventies.

(Footnote continued from previous page)

the academic labour market itself. In the United Kingdom and the United States, there have been wide variations in the proportion of graduates obtaining university posts. What happens is that an initial shortage of graduate manpower stimulates the expansion of higher education. This increases the demands of the educational system on its own output and exacerbates the shortage in the rest of the economy. Subsequently, the increased capacity of the higher education system leads to a reduction in its own rate of growth and an increased output of graduates reaches the labour market. University recruitment is thus reduced just as more graduates become available. As the educational system exacerbated the original shortage of graduates, so it now magnifies the subsequent surplus. (See Gareth Williams: "University recruitment, 1969 and 1971", Social Science Research Council Newsletter (London, December 1972)).

[1] Cornmarket salary survey, 1965-71 (London, Cornmarket Press, 1972). See also "The graduate labour market" by Gareth Williams in Three Banks Review, September 1973.

[2] Department of Education and Science: Survey of earnings of qualified manpower in England and Wales, 1966-67, Statistics of Education, Special Series, No. 3 (London, HMSO, 1971).

According to the 1971 and 1972 reports of the
Universities Central Council on Admissions, the number of
applications to universities has gone down. At the same
time, there are indications of changes in the patterns of
employment of graduates. Thus, while the numbers of those
entering industry declined between 1968 and 1971, more
graduates have turned towards public service activities and
commerce. There has also been an increase in the numbers
opting for vocational studies after graduation.[1] Many of
those who withdrew their applications to universities during
the admission process - their numbers rose sharply in 1972
- may have made a similar choice.

In the Netherlands, a commission charged with
forecasting the supply and demand for graduates predicted
that by 1980 there would be a surplus of 5,000 graduates,
mainly among social scientists. It has now become clear
that this figure will be reached much earlier and will
include graduates in engineering and the natural sciences.
In mid-June 1972, some 900 graduates were registered with
the employment service as unemployed and some 200 as
employed but seeking work more fitted to their training.
This does not represent a high percentage of the total, but
is a cause of concern because there are indications that the
surplus is not a transitory phenomenon but reflects a
structural imbalance. Industry and the universities place
the blame on each other; according to the former, the
expectation level of graduates is too high, with the
universities still leading their students to believe that
they are an élite group; according to the latter, industry
has fluctuated violently in its demand for graduates. There
is also an ideological mismatch in that a fair number of the
new graduates are hostile to private enterprise, which
accordingly does not have unlimited patience in helping such
people to settle down in employment.[2]

In France there is less unanimity on employment
difficulties of graduates. Although statistical information
necessary to determine whether there has been a
deterioration in the employment opportunities of university
graduates is lacking, there is growing concern. Over the
last decade there has been a large increase in the number of
students at all levels of education. As in other countries,
pressures towards social change, towards democratisation and
modernisation of higher education have brought about a
spectacular growth in the number of students enrolled in
universities - there were about 700,000 students in France
in 1972, twice as many as in 1965 (the sudden decrease

----

[1] University Grants Committee: First employment of
university graduates, 1970-71 (London, HMSO, 1972).

[2] P.G.M. de Kleijn: "Unemployment among graduates" in
Higher Education and Research in the Netherlands, Vol. 17,
No. 1, 1973.

reported in 1973 may be a result of graduate employment
problems). The rapid increase in enrolment in universities
and higher educational establishments was largely the result
of the liberalisation of entry during the late 1960s. This
has led to expectations in the minds of large numbers of
young people that the labour market may not be able to
satisfy. Yet, as has been pointed out in a report by the
Commission des affaires culturelles, familiales et sociales,
there are ambiguities in considering open access to higher
education as being unquestionably a liberalising policy.
Although university entry is non-competitive and enrolment
virtually unlimited (apart from the "Grandes Ecoles"), a
selection takes place at the end of the first year,
indicated by the high rate of failures at examinations -
over 40 per cent.[1] According to the Commission's report, the
economic, social and human costs of this device are
considerable.

At the same time, a good deal of innovation and
experiment in higher education has been made possible by the
"Loi d'orientation" of 1968 such as, to mention but a few,
greater autonomy for the universities and the creation of
multidisciplinary streams, replacement of the conventional
lecture system with its large audiences by individual and
collective work in small groups, new methods of testing
knowledge and an orientation and guidance system designed to
help students more effectively in appropriate academic and
career choices. For this purpose, "information cells" have
been created in the universities comprising teaching staff
of secondary and higher educational institutions as well as
guidance personnel.[2] Closer university-industry-civil
service ties are also advocated in the way of work periods
for students and faculty members, consultantships for
academic staff, joint study programme development and
systems similar to the "sandwich courses" operating in the
United Kingdom (which alternate study at the university with
work in industry).

In the official view, the problem does not lie in the
number of students and graduates, which at all levels
corresponds to the targets of the VIth Plan, but in their
distribution over the various disciplines and kinds of
degree course. Thus, the rapid development of the service
industries, of communications, of management techniques and
of other fields has created a mismatch between study
programmes and the employment opportunities available.

However, two categories of French graduates appear so
far to be experiencing little difficulty in finding suitable
jobs. These are graduates from the Grandes Ecoles, which
----

[1] OECD: Reviews of national policies for education:
France (Paris, 1971), p. 70.

[2] Le Monde (Paris), 20 February 1973, p. 10.

are highly selective and in a sense stand above the universities, and those from the University Institutes of Technology (Instituts Universitaires de Technologie - IUTs), first established in 1966, the standard of which may be regarded as slightly lower than that of the regular universities. Both institutions, although very different, provide vocational and specialised education, in the case of the Grandes Ecoles at a very high professional level. They both comprise a very small part of the higher education sector, about 4 per cent each in 1972. In both the success rate is high, the proportion of graduates to the number enrolled being over 90 per cent, much higher than in the universities.

Acceptance by one of the Grandes Ecoles carries a good chance of a senior post in the public sector and their graduates also have little difficulty in finding suitable employment elsewhere. While the number of university students increased by 33 per cent between 1968 and 1972, the number in the Grandes Ecoles increased by only 20 per cent.

The IUTs are in some respects the opposite extreme from the Grandes Ecoles. Entry is at the moment restricted by the availability of places, but they are not geared to an academic or social élite; rather they cater for young people who expect to become middle-level technicians. However, their graduates also have so far experienced little difficulty in entering the labour market. According to a recent study by the "Centre for Study and Research on Qualifications" (Centre d'Etudes et de Recherches sur les Qualifications), the proportion of IUT graduates in search of suitable employment 21 months after graduation was 2.4 per cent. It is hard to relate this figure to that of university graduates as no comparable studies have been made, but it undoubtedly reflects a much greater success in placement.

One of the countries in which there is no immediate evidence of serious graduate employment problems, but where there are fears for the future, is the Federal Republic of Germany. The number of graduates in relation to the age group is lower than in most other highly industrialised countries: there are about 66 students per 10,000 population compared with 136 in Sweden, 128 in France and 97 in Italy. Yet between 1960 and 1969 the number of students grew by almost 50 per cent.

The only categories of graduates for which there appear to be employment problems at present are chemists and to some extent physicists. The blame for the imbalance is usually attributed to incorrect manpower forecasting. It is estimated that, if the output of chemistry graduates continues to grow at the present rate, by 1979 it will be twice the number of vacancies in industry for which a chemistry degree is relevant.

It is interesting to note that in both the United
Kingdom and the United States, the market for chemistry
graduates deteriorated some years before it did for
graduates of other specialisations.[1] One reason for this is
that the nature of the chemical industry is such that when
new materials are being developed, such as polymer plastics,
hormone-based insecticides and weedkillers, vast numbers of
highly qualified people are required for the basic research.
When, however, the new product has been perfected, its
routine production requires far fewer qualified personnel.
Meanwhile, the scientists who have carried out the basic
research have become so specialised that it is not easy for
them to transfer to some other line of research.

While the present employment situation of other
graduates in the Federal Republic of Germany is not
alarming, there seems to be a good deal of concern for the
future. Three recent studies, though differing considerably
in detail, agree that on present trends, the output of
graduates in the 1970s will grow very rapidly: in 1980 it
is likely to be 80 per cent higher than in 1968, and the
proportion of female graduates is expected to double. If
present patterns of academic career choice continue without
correctives, serious imbalances are likely to result. The
forecasts, however, vary considerably both as to the fields
and to the proportions of imbalance; in general, an over-
supply of graduates in the humanities and the social
sciences is expected, while the demand for graduates in
technical subjects is thought likely to grow. Currently,
however, the number of the latter has dropped (an opposite
trend can be observed in the German Democratic Republic,
where the number of graduates in the technical sciences
during the same period has grown[2]).

However, it must be added that there is also some
scepticism in the Federal Republic about the validity of
such projections. Many people believe that in a buoyant
economy, the labour market is capable of adapting itself to
very substantial changes in the qualification mix of those
leaving the educational system. Reference is frequently
made to a pilot study on the employment of political science
graduates carried out by the Max Planck Institute for

----

[1] In the United States, unemployment among new chemists
doubled from 5.1 per cent in 1970 to 10.3 per cent in 1971.
The unemployment rate for new chemical engineers rose from
3.4 per cent in 1970 to 12.8 per cent in 1971. At the same
time, chemists' starting salaries in 1971 were down 6.7 per
cent from 1970 levels. (Chemical and Engineering News,
Washington, 1 November 1971, p. 26.)

[2] Bundesminister für innerdeutsche Beziehungen: Bericht
der Bundesregierung und Materialen zur Lage der Nation
(Bonn, 1971), p. 202.

Educational Research in 1969[1] to examine how graduates in a
new discipline fared on a labour market which was reportedly
unfavourable to the social sciences and in which there was
no current demand for this type of degree. In the event,
most of these graduates were found to have obtained
employment - one-third in teaching, one-fifth in public
administration and the rest in various private sector jobs,
all at salaries comparable to those of other graduates. The
study also found that, once a particular post had been
filled by a political science graduate, the employer tended
to specify this degree as necessary for subsequent recruits
to that post. However, other studies have interpreted this
and similar evidence as showing an increasing tendency for
people to be over-qualified for the posts they hold. One-
third of all the jobs analysed in a recent survey could have
been filled by persons with higher technical college
education (Fachhochschulen) rather than a university
degree.[2] What this may mean is that provided an economy is
operating at or near full employment, graduates as well as
secondary and technical school leavers are absorbed into the
labour force somehow and only detailed job analysis can
determine whether their qualifications are actually "needed"
for the tasks they are performing.

One problem which is receiving growing attention in
the German Federal Republic concerns the measures taken to
limit study in certain subjects. At practically all
universities, there is a "numerus clausus" in medicine,
dentistry and pharmacy, while in certain universities there
are local restrictions in a few other disciplines. The
restricted entry into the former studies is creating a
shortage on the labour market which is likely to grow.
While the "numerus clausus" is considered contrary to
article 12 of the Constitution, which guarantees freedom of
choice of the institution and the subject of study, this
freedom is in practice restricted by such factors as
absorption capacity, financial resources, structural
deficiencies, etc.[3] The "numerus clausus", although
considered a temporary measure, cannot by itself solve the
problem of over-crowded universities. Many students waiting
for admission to restricted subjects enrol in unrestricted
faculties, thus shifting the burden on capacity elsewhere;
in 1970, over half of all medical students had previously

----

[1] D. Hartung, R. Nuthmann, W.D. Winterhager: Polito-
logen im Beruf (Stuttgart, Ernst Klett Verlag, 1970).

[2] K.M. Kuntz: Hochschulabsolventen im Beruf (Cologne,
Institut für Sozioökonomische Strukturforschung GmbH, 1972).

[3] However, according to a recent ruling of the
Constitutional Court, a limited "numerus clausus" is
permitted in order to keep numbers at a level which would
ensure proper education for students.

studied another subject.[1] In spite of plans for university expansion, the shortage of places is likely to persist considering that, by 1980, 45 per cent of the 18 year old age group is expected to qualify for admission to higher education. Alternative channels of education, vocationally-oriented and of shorter duration will therefore be needed to relieve the pressure on universities and to help reduce the present drop-out rates.

The Socialist countries

In the Socialist countries of Eastern Europe the increased demand for higher education which, as elsewhere, reflects people's rising educational aspirations, exceeds the number of available places in most subjects. But there has been no explosion of higher education because expansion has been controlled in relation to forecast requirements for various types of graduates and specialists in the medium and long-term plans. These forecasts put an upper limit on admission to higher educational establishments. It appears that in general, requirements for graduate manpower are foreseen several years ahead with sufficient accuracy, if allowance is made for rolling adjustments taking account of periodic revisions of the perspective plans.[2] However, long-term estimates are difficult to make, as in other economies, owing to unforeseen developments in science and technology, growth factors and changes in the structure of various branches of the economy. As an example, the introduction of economic reforms during the 1960s led to an unforeseen demand for economists, management and marketing specialists, and in Hungary (as in the Federal Republic of Germany and the United Kingdom) the demand for chemists was over-estimated.

This method of relating higher education to labour market needs obviously avoids the emergence of graduate unemployment because every graduate produced has, in principle, a job already waiting for him. However, it is not always the case that graduates accept the jobs planned for them and in a situation of general shortage there seem to be cases where graduates, for example doctors and teachers, especially women, prefer to wait for jobs in the large cities rather than accept immediately vacancies in small towns or remote country districts.

----

[1] It has been suggested that it would be more rational if those who are queuing up for medical studies could be acquiring practical experience through employment in hospitals instead of cluttering up non-medical faculties in the universities.

[2] V. Zhamin: "Forecasting the Level of Education", Voprosy ekonomik (Moscow, 1972), No. 9, pp. 24-33.

The avoidance of graduate employment problems has not, of course, been achieved without cost and this cost has been the increasing competition for university entry. In Poland, for example, there were in 1970 eight applicants for every place in art and architecture schools, three applications per place in universities and 1.5 applicants per place in polytechnics. In the USSR there are three to four applications for each place in full-time study. In Hungary the average number of applicants per university place is about 2.5 and the number admitted has increased only by about 20 per cent since 1960. No substantial change is foreseen in the number of students admitted to all the institutions and faculties of higher education until 1980; at the same time, it is planned to increase the student population in vocational secondary schools to meet the needs of industry for technicians and skilled workers.[1]

In Romania pressure for entry to university appears to be even higher, figures of thirty applicants per place in one subject being quoted. Because of limits in the capacity of the higher educational institutions and the increasing number of qualified secondary school leavers, standards of admission have become more and more severe. Through vocational orientation and guidance, applicants are helped to choose other careers. In Czechoslovakia, for instance, there are various incentive schemes such as additional scholarships to attract students to educational institutions which have empty places.

Table 12 shows that, whereas in most Western Europen countries enrolments in higher education grew at more than twice the rate of enrolments in secondary education, in all the East European countries the relative growth rate was less than double. In fact, the contrast is probably even greater in practice as the Eastern European figures include enrolments in part-time higher education and extra-mural courses which appear to have grown more rapidly than full-time enrolments. In the USSR almost half of all students who graduated in 1970 had obtained their diplomas through evening and correspondence courses taken concurrently with employment.[2] Similarly in the German Democratic Republic where industrial and other undertakings are required by law to help their workers, especially women, to pursue this type of study, about one-quarter of all students were in 1970 enrolled on a part-time or extra-mural basis.

----

[1] A. Kiss and J. Timar: "Supply of qualified labour in the Hungarian national economy", Acta Oeconomica (Budapest, 1971), Vol. 6(3), p. 211.

[2] USSR: Central Office of Statistics: Narodnoye Khoziaistvo SSR v 1970 godu (Moscow, Statistika, 1971), p. 645.

Table 12.   Average annual percentage rate of
growth of enrolments in secondary education and
higher education in European countries
1960-1968 and 1968-1971

	1960-1968			1968-1972
	Secondary (A)	Higher (B)	$\frac{B}{A}$	Higher
Austria	3.0	3.1	1.03	
Belgium	3.5	7.5	2.14	
Bulgaria	3.0	5.8	1.93	
Czechoslovakia	2.9	1.2	0.41	
Denmark	1.9	7.5	3.95	
Finland	4.2	11.1	2.64	
France	6.2	12.5	2.02	10.9 (1968-1972)
Federal Republic of Germany	3.1	6.5	2.10	
German Democratic Republic	(n.a.)	1.5	-	11.5 (1969-1971)
Hungary	5.6	7.5	1.34	-3.2 (1966-1971)
Italy	6.2	10.2	1.65	14.0
Netherlands	2.0	9.8	4.90	
Norway	5.1	12.8	2.51	
Poland	6.3	7.5	1.19	3.2 (1968-1972)
Romania	7.5	4.2	0.56	
Sweden	6.9	15.8	2.29	
United Kingdom	-	11.8	(11.8)	5.3 (1968-1972)
USSR	6.9	6.9	1.0	3.5 (1968-1972)
Yugoslavia	8.5	7.5	0.88	

Source: UNESCO, Statistical yearbook (Paris, 1971).

In these countries, though practices may vary in
detail, students usually finance their studies by taking a
scholarship which is awarded on condition that they enter a
specific employment for a determined period after
graduating. In some countries, such as Poland and Romania,
students holding scholarships who wish to be released from
their commitment may do so either by repaying the sum
equivalent to the scholarship granted to them during their
studies or be "bought out" by another employer.[1] An
alternative for students in Romania is to avoid any
commitment about future employment by paying the fees
themselves (these are in any case heavily subsidised); it
appears that an increasing number of students are taking
this option. In some countries, the relatively tight labour
market for graduates has meant that such "uncommitted"
graduates are particularly sought after by certain busy
industries.

As in many Western countries, in the USSR a large
proportion of the scientific personnel - over one-third - is
employed by universities and other higher educational
institutions. The expansion of these institutions during
the last few years has resulted in an increase in the number
of students, particularly in science and technology.
However, one of the problems is reported to be that "the
planning of the training, distribution and utilisation of
specialists does not fully correspond to the requirements of
the national economy".[2] Constant efforts are therefore made
to reflect the latest achievements in science and technology
in study programmes and curricula in order to meet the needs
of science and production. Higher educational institutions
are also called upon to reinforce their ties with industrial
and agricultural undertakings and research institutions and
thus give more attention to solving urgent scientific and
technical problems. One of the tasks of the recently
created Council on Higher Schools under the USSR Ministry of
Higher and Specialised Secondary Education is to look into
the long-range planning of the training, distribution and
utilisation of specialists. Shortages of highly qualified
manpower are particularly acute in newly-developed
industrial areas.

This problem of planning and producing the number and
types of graduate required while allowing sufficient
flexibility for the changing needs of the economy, is also
reported from Poland. A recently published report by an
expert committee on the educational system containing

---

[1] Polish People's Republic: Act of 25 February 1964
regarding the employment of persons graduating from higher
education establishments.

[2] CPSU Central Committee and USSR Council of Ministers:
"On measures for the further improvement of higher education
in the country", Pravda (Moscow), 30 July 1972, pp. 1-2.

proposals for reforms warns against too narrow
specialisation and underlines the importance for educational
institutions of keeping up with scientific and technical
progress.[1]

What may appear at first sight to be a fairly rigid
system is in practice rendered flexible by arrangements for
late entry into higher education by mature students and by
the widespread provision of part-time higher education. For
instance in the USSR, there is an alternative entry scheme
for workers, mostly between the ages of 23 and 30 (the upper
limit is 35), many of whom are paid for by their
undertaking; for these workers there is a special
preparatory course of one year to bring their general
education up to a level with that of direct entrants; these
mature students may make up to 20 per cent of the total
enrolment.

The widespread system of part-time higher education in
the Socialist countries was originally conceived as a way of
helping those who had not had proper opportunities in their
youth. Now it serves also as a fall-back for educated young
people who have not obtained a place in full-time courses.
Competition for entry is less severe - 1.5 applicants to 1
place is mentioned in some countries; the number of places
is less rigidly controlled and courses are opened up or
closed down in accordance with the local demand, with extra-
mural courses being run at remotely situated factories where
there is sufficient demand. The student accepts no
commitment to his employing undertaking, which, for its
part, has however to give him a prescribed amount of time
off for study and, when he qualifies, to place him in a job
corresponding to his new qualifications (if one exists in
the undertaking). In principle, a degree acquired by part-
time study has parity with one acquired by full-time study;
in practice, this form of higher education is reported to be
most successful in occupations where practical experience
counts for more than theoretical knowledge.

There is not the same differential between the
salaries of graduates and the wages of other workers as
exists in Western European countries. In general, the
starting salary of a graduate in his mid-twenties is lower
than that of a highly-skilled worker of the same age who has
already been working for five years or more. In the German
Democratic Republic the average starting salary of graduates
in 1970 was about M.750 per month, which is equivalent to
the average wage of a worker or employee. In Hungary it has
been calculated that if total earnings are spread over total
working years a graduate does not catch up with a skilled
worker until he reaches the age of about 40.
----

[1] Polish People's Republic: _Założenia i tezy raportu o
stanie oswiaty_ (Warsaw, February 1973).

Teachers' salaries provide another indicator. Although teachers are not the best paid intellectual workers in any country, a comparison of their earnings with those of production workers has some significance. In Hungary in 1970 the average pay of teachers was only 95 per cent of that of industrial workers. In several other Eastern European countries, it is even lower: 90 per cent of average industrial earnings in Bulgaria, 85 per cent in Czechoslovakia and Poland[1] and 78 per cent in the Soviet Union.

In general, therefore, social policy in Eastern European countries has tended to limit the financial advantages of being a graduate. However, even if the incentive to enter higher education may not be foremost an economic one, graduates still enjoy considerable social status and prestige and have a greater chance of promotion to senior posts in government and industry than their less well educated counterparts.

An examination of the issues

This survey of the employment situation for graduates in a number of European countries has revealed a number of interesting points.

Rates of expansion

First there is clearly, as might be expected, a relationship between the rate of growth of higher education and the ease with which graduates enter the labour market.

It should be emphasised that the relationship is with the growth rate of the output of graduates and not with either the level of output or with the stock of highly qualified manpower as a proportion of the labour force. As table 12 has shown, growth has been much more explosive in some countries than others. During the 1960s the rate of growth of enrolments varied between 1.2 per cent per year in Czechoslovakia and 15.8 per cent in Sweden. The United States had a proportion of graduates in the labour force and a rate of output of graduates in 1960 as high as most European countries in 1970, yet the early 1960s in the United States, as in Western European countries, was a period of great shortage of graduates. What the United States shared with Western Europe, as table 12 shows, was a very rapid rate of growth of enrolments in higher education, much more rapid than enrolment growth in secondary education. In general the growth rate is considerably

----

[1] Because of a shortage of teachers in Poland salary scales are at present being reviewed.

higher in the countries which have tried to relate their provision of higher education to the individual demand for places than it is in countries which have related their growth to estimated manpower needs.

However, we must also bear in mind that, while the rates of growth we have been examining are those throughout a decade or more, it is only in the past two or three years that the employment problems of graduates have begun to attract the attention of policy makers. Since the rapid growth rate in enrolments occurred throughout the 1960s, whereas unemployment only began to arise at the end of the decade, it is not sufficient simply to claim that over-rapid growth of higher education leads to graduate employment difficulties. Furthermore the growth rate in those countries where such problems occur has not been uniform, particularly in the most recent years. In Italy, and until very recently in France, educational growth has continued at its explosive rate, but in the United Kingdom and Sweden, as in the United States, it has slowed down considerably.

Unfortunately, on the basis of the information currently available, any further suggestions about the relationship between educational expansion and the labour market on the basis of international comparisons must remain highly speculative. It would, however, be useful if such speculation would encourage concerted international action to collect the information necessary to test the various assumptions.

What more then can be said other than that a rapid rate of growth of secondary and higher education seems more likely to lead to graduate employment problems than a slower rate? What determines the rate at which the economy can absorb qualified manpower and why do some countries seem to be able to absorb it at a more rapid rate than others?

The effect of fluctuations

It seems reasonable to assume that one of the factors that determines the rate at which graduates can be absorbed into the labour force is the rate at which jobs in general become available. If a man with a primary education retires from the labour force there may be few social tensions and probably some economic gain involved in replacing him with a secondary school leaver or even a graduate. If, however, attempts are made to replace him before he retires, serious personnel problems and tensions may arise. One of the problems in manpower planning is to create career structures and promotion and retirement policies that lead to stability in the demand, or of the growth in demand, for people with various qualifications.

One type of cyclical fluctuation arises if, for whatever reason, there is an initial shortage of qualified manpower in one sector of the economy or in the economy generally. This is likely to result in a period of high recruitment while the shortage is being overcome. Subsequently, although there may be a continuing long-run growth in the demand for that type of manpower, the rate of growth of the demand must be less than was needed to overcome the original shortage.[1] Thus the rate of growth of the educational system that was required to overcome the original shortage cannot be sustained in the long run. Moreover, the dynamics of age structures exacerbate the problem. One result of previous rapid increases in recruitment is that there is now an unbalanced age structure with large numbers of young people. Thus, the average retirement rate in relation to the stock is low and this again puts a brake on demand for qualified manpower. Meanwhile, of course, because of the earlier high recruitment, attitudes and expectations of students and graduates regarding future careers have been raised to an unrealistically high level. Expectations and attitudes are likely to be more realistic when there are reliable manpower predictions and a system of career advice which can anticipate trends and developments in the graduate employment market.

Perhaps the most dramatic example of this mechanism occurred in many African countries where, at the time of independence, the qualified manpower stock was extremely low. This meant that for the first generation after independence, educational qualifications were a passport to extremely rapid career advancement. Immediately subsequent generations were faced with a situation in which they had extremely high career expectations as a result of their educational qualifications. At the same time, their real opportunities were reduced because senior posts were largely filled by people with many years of active life ahead of them. Clearly in Europe no such extreme situation exists. However, analysis of the age structure of almost any hierarchical career reveals a bunching of people at certain ages indicating fluctuations in past recruitment and probably fluctuations in future recruitment patterns.

Such recruitment fluctuations may well be generated and can certainly be magnified by demographic distortions resulting from an unbalanced age structure of the whole

----

[1] This can be readily illustrated formally with the famous "Tinbergen model of education and the economy" (see OECD: _Econometric models of education_, (Paris, 1965)). During the "transition period" when initial manpower shortages are overcome, either qualified manpower must be temporarily imported while the shortage is overcome and then expelled as soon as the national education system has expanded sufficiently, or the educational system must temporarily expand at a more rapid rate than long-run equilibrium will sustain, meanwhile denuding the rest of the economy of qualified manpower during the transition period.

population.   In   most   Western   European   countries,   for
example, except the Federal Republic of Germany and Austria,
there was a sharp rise in the birth rate during the year
1946 which only slowly declined in the early 1950s. During
the 1960s this birth bulge was passing through the higher
education system and was partly responsible for the very
rapid rise in enrolments.   By the end of the decade,
graduates from these swollen birth cohorts were beginning to
enter the labour force with high level qualifications.

        Eastern   European   countries   did not experience sharp
birth rate bulges in the late 1940s like those of Western
Europe.   More   importantly, however, as has been shown, the
growth of higher education in Eastern Europe was linked
closely to estimated needs for qualified manpower. Thus the
effect of demographic fluctuations was to vary the rate of
competition for entry to higher education rather than the
rate of growth of enrolments.

        Another structural feature of manpower systems that
can both generate fluctuations and magnify those generated
for other reasons is the "acceleration" effect of the
education system itself. The cycle can be considered to
start with an initial perception of a need for more
qualified manpower. The educational system expands in order
to overcome this shortage.[1] The immediate effect of the
educational expansion is an increased demand for teachers.
If the educational sector succeeds in acquiring them[2], this
exacerbates the manpower shortage in the rest of the economy
and makes the possession of a high level qualification even
more attractive. In a few years, however, the increase in
enrolments results in an increased output of graduates who
enter the labour force and overcome the immediate manpower
shortage.   This lessens the attractiveness of educational
qualifications and the pressure for expansion is lessened.
Recruitment of teachers is reduced, thus releasing even more
qualified manpower to the rest of the economy and the whole
cycle is reversed.

        Clearly the operation of this accelerator in the 1960s
was accentuated by the demographic movements already noted.

        Another aspect of educational and manpower structures
which complicates education/labour market relationships is
that it is a complex lagged system. There are behavioural
----

        [1] The expansion may come about as a result of
educational planning linked to manpower forecasts, or it may
occur because of increased demand for higher education by
school leavers who perceive good employment opportunities
for those with high level qualifications.

        [2] An econometric analysis of such fluctuations in the
United States is contained in The market for college-trained
manpower, by Richard Freeman (Cambridge, Mass., Harvard
University Press, 1971).

lags because it takes some time for a shortage or surplus to be perceived, during which time it may get worse and there are structural lags because any educational process takes time to complete. An increase in engineering education on account of a perceived shortage will require a minimum of three or four years before an increased output of engineers results - and possibly much longer, if new facilities have to be created and teachers recruited. It is a well-known characteristic of all such lagged systems that they result in fluctuations. The problem is to establish an information and control system which reduces the fluctuations to an acceptable level.

Finally, one structural feature that went strangely unnoticed during the period of manpower shortages of the early 1960s was the mechanics of manpower substitution. During shortages of qualified manpower, employers find ways of substituting less well qualified manpower with perhaps some loss of productivity. Forecasts of manpower needs rarely took this into account, in fact rather the reverse, by allowing for an upgrading of labour force qualifications. However, it is difficult in practice to remove the less qualified people as soon as new graduates appear. Not unnaturally, those already in the posts try to maintain their position and they are aided in this by the fact that for a variety of historical, economic and institutional reasons, highly qualified manpower often has very considerable security of tenure. At the same time the junior employees, better qualified than their seniors, may resent seeing their avenues for promotion blocked.

Students' expectations

It is often suggested in countries which are experiencing graduate employment difficulties that new graduates must revise their employment expectations downwards as if it was utterly irrational of graduates to have such high expectations. However, very little research has been conducted to find out why such high expectations were formed. It is certainly a likely hypothesis that the most important reason was the qualified manpower shortage of the 1960s, full employment and relatively high salary growth, combined with inadequate guidance to warn pupils and students against projecting the existing situation too far into the future.

One fundamental reason for the persistent tendency of higher education enrolment to outstrip the economic demand for the products of higher education may lie in the interaction between the method of higher education subsidy, the basing of criteria for the provision of places on demand by individual students and the adjustment mechanisms of the labour market, which prevent graduate salaries from adjusting rapidly to changed market conditions. This is a very large subject, but the effect of such a situation is to ensure firstly, that on average the private rate of return to education is much above the social rate and secondly, that the perceived returns of those who do succeed in securing employment are (as the example of Italy has shown) very high.

Clearly, the larger the differential between graduate and non-graduate salaries, the greater the extent to which the provision of higher education is geared to individual demand for places and the greater the subsidy to individuals undertaking that education, the more likely such a situation is to arise. In Eastern European countries, graduate salaries are not high in relation to those of ordinary workers but perhaps more important, the provision of places is based not on the demands of individual students but on estimated manpower needs.

However, this solution has its own problems. As has already been shown, it intensifies the competition for entry into higher education. What this means in effect is that "selection" takes place before higher education entry rather than after. Even so, this has some advantages, inasmuch as there are both economic and humanitarian reasons for not delaying selection until after people have invested heavily in a particular specialisation and it becomes extremely difficult for them to change directions.

As previously indicated, one view of graduate unemployment is that it is merely one aspect of general unemployment; if general unemployment did not exist, neither would unemployed graduates. In one sense, of course, this is true by definition, but in another sense it evades the issues. One concern in some countries is that unemployment of qualified manpower has been rising more rapidly than that of other categories. More importantly, unemployment of graduates is economically more wasteful than unemployment of untrained manpower in that the resources devoted to the training of graduates could, in other circumstances, have been devoted to the creation of physical capital which could be used to generate employment. While, therefore, graduate unemployment is merely one aspect of the general employment situation, it does have important resource allocation aspects which make its solution important independently of that of unemployment generally.

One aspect of this issue is, however, a little more subtle. In a situation where some unemployment exists, there may well be a tendency for highly qualified manpower to be substituted for less qualified workers because their possession of a qualification is evidence of greater natural ability. This means that the relative disadvantages of not having educational qualifications become ever greater, thus increasing the demand for such qualifications. Meanwhile, however, the possession of educational qualifications ceases to be a passport to high level employment and becomes merely a ticket in the "lottery" for what high-level employment is available.

Imbalances in the educational system

So far we have discussed the interactions between the educational system and the labour market in terms of over-all quantitative imbalances brought about by structural, institutional or behavioural features of the educational system or the labour market as a whole.

There is, however, another widely held view which is that the problem is not due to over-all imbalance but the failure of the educational system to reflect the needs of the labour market. There are, broadly speaking, two main strands to this argument. The first is that the subjects taught in higher education institutions are inappropriate to labour market needs.[1] Attention is drawn to the high proportion and rapid growth of students in literary subjects and social sciences. Table 13 shows that in general in Western European countries, science and technology students comprised between a third and a half of total students in 1968 and grew less rapidly than the student body as a whole. In Eastern Europe on the other hand, science students comprised well over half the total and their numbers grew at least as rapidly as those studying other subjects.

The second line of argument is that the educational system - the universities are often singled out for special opprobrium in this respect - is motivated not by the real needs of society as a whole, but by academic incentives, and sometimes its own vested interests. This results, for example, in graduates with little interest in the social values necessary to economic growth, or in university research undertaken for intellectual pleasure or for the furtherance of personal careers, rather than to solve the practical problems of the physical and social world.

----

[1] An example is the recent "Memorandum of the Confederation of British Industries to Education and Arts Subcommittee of House of Commons Expenditure Committee" which states: "Notwithstanding the slowdown in growth of total post-graduate numbers at the universities we support some further shift towards supplementing the research content of post-graduate degree work with courses of relevance to industry (increasingly so in the European context), believing that the value of these students as potential employees would be enhanced by virtue of increased flexibility of attitude and a wider knowledge of the functions of industry. This is consistent with a theme which, although not universally accepted in academic quarters, has been advocated on a number of occasions, at least as a subject for experimentation." (Supplement to the CBI Education and Training Bulletin, May 1973.)

Table 13.   European countries: Distribution
of students and rate of growth of higher
education by subject group during the 1960s

	Science		Non-Science	
	% in 1968	% p.a. growth in 1960s	% in 1968	% p.a. growth in 1960s
Austria	49.4	2.4	50.6	4.1
Belgium	47.2	1.5	52.8	2.4
Bulgaria	61.2	5.0	38.8	8.8
Czechoslovakia	68.6	2.9	31.4	-1.8
Denmark	34.5	10.8	65.5	9.4
Finland	34.4	11.5	65.6	11.0
France	43.3	10.8	56.7	14.6
Federal Republic of Germany	47.4	5.1	52.6	7.4
German Democratic Republic	57.3	0.4	42.7	3.5
Hungary	69.0	7.5	31.0	7.3
Italy	38.2	11.5	61.8	9.4
Netherlands	49.2	8.1	50.8	9.9
Norway	39.6	8.8	60.4	16.2
Poland	60.3	7.2	39.7	7.6
Romania	51.0	5.9	49.0	14.5
Sweden	32.4	11.4	67.6	18.5
United Kingdom	37.5	8.4	62.5	14.4

Source: UNESCO: Statistical yearbook (Paris, 1970).

Both of these contentions are much harder to prove or disprove than claims about over-all quantitative imbalances. It is, for example, extremely difficult to claim unequivocally that science or technology graduates are in fact more useful to society than graduates in foreign languages, social sciences, economics and law. Thus, in the United Kingdom during the 1950s and 1960s, there was very considerable concern about a shortage of scientists and technologists. Consequently, science and technology places in universities were created at a much more rapid rate than in other subjects. By the mid-1960s, this concern turned to alarm when it was discovered that a decreasing proportion of secondary school children were choosing science options and many measures were proposed to reverse this "swing from science".

When, however, the results of the first national earnings survey held in 1967 became known at the end of the decade[1], it was seen that the lifetime earnings of arts and social science graduates (which in a market economy are likely to bear some relationship to productivity) were considerably above those of people with science degrees. From a private point of view certainly, and from a social point of view probably, therefore, schoolchildren were making the right choice in ignoring the advice of the planners.[2] Subsequently, another official publiciation[3] showed that unemployment of scientists and technologists had been rising throughout the 1960s during the period of believed shortage. Clearly, this single example from one country needs to be examined more closely and in the light of evidence from other countries; it is quoted here merely to show that it is not self-evident that rapid expansion of non-science studies is a major cause of graduate employment problems.

It should also be remembered that the cost of education in science and technology is in general much higher than in social sciences and literary subjects. In the wider context, therefore, of the efficient allocation of society's resources as a whole, it is less "wasteful" to have too much provision of education in the latter subjects than to have too much science and technology in which extended training often results in specialisation useful

----

[1] Department of Education and Science: Statistics of Education, Special Series, No. 3, op. cit.

[2] See Gannicott and Blaug, "Manpower forecasting: A science lobby in action", Higher Education Review (London), Autumn 1969.

[3] Department of Trade and Industry: Persons with qualifications in engineering, technology and science, 1959-1968 (London, HMSO, 1971).

only for a very narrow range of jobs, or for transient
needs. On the other hand, a background in social sciences,
economy and law is certainly useful for a wider range of
professional, administrative and managerial posts.

A related complaint concerns the lack of career advice
and general counselling for students. Certainly the
inadequacy of career information and counselling services
for academic streams of secondary schools and in higher
education is one of the marked weaknesses of the educational
systems of most countries of Western Europe. There is much
evidence that educationalists and policy makers are becoming
increasingly aware of the need for professional counselling
services. In December 1972, for example, a British
Parliamentary Committee of Inquiry in Higher Education
Expenditure called for the establishment of a National
Careers Advisory Service.[1] Many other countries have or are
setting up similar services. The need for better
orientation services is also expressed in several Eastern
European countries.

It is also possible to claim that the labour market is
inappropriately organised to absorb the output of the higher
educational system. On this view, it is less a matter of
anticipating the number of jobs traditionally occupied by
graduates - as if occupational roles remained constant
forever - than of knowing how the labour market adjusts to
graduates' qualifications and what the economic and social
effects of these qualifications are. Reference has already
been made to a study of the occupational situation of
political scientists, a new kind of graduate for whose
qualifications there had previously been no specific demand
on the labour market. Similar studies could usefully be
made on how graduates in other new disciplines, particularly
the social sciences, use their knowledge and skills or widen
the range of their applicability and what are the social and
institutional impediments, if any, which hamper utilisation
of the qualifications. At the same time, it would be useful
to know how new needs arising out of innovations in
technology, science and the organisation of work or out of
new problem areas, such as environmental protection or rapid
urban growth, affect the occupational structure and the mix
of output from the higher educational system.

Some suggestions for educational and labour market policy

The provision of secondary and higher education on a
basis that is socially equitable between all groups in
----

[1] Department of Education and Science: First Report of
the Expenditure Committee, Session 1972/73: Further and
Higher Education (London, HMSO, December 1972).

society and between present and future generations and is at
the same time economically efficient is one of the most
complex social problems of the present age. It is therefore
hardly surprising that so far no country seems to have found
an entirely satisfactory way of achieving this desirable
end.

In the Socialist countries of Eastern Europe, the aim
has been to relate the provision of places in full-time
higher education closely to estimated manpower needs and to
commit employers to take the numbr of graduates allowed for
in their manpower plans. This has certainly prevented the
emergence of major graduate employment problems but it has
meant increased competition for places. These countries
have attempted to overcome their problems, partly by student
counselling services, partly by the provision of an
extensive system of part-time and correspondence education
and partly by wage policies that try to prevent the
emergence of wide salary differentials between graduates and
other groups of workers. Yet do those who undertake part-
time study have the same career chances as those who are
able to secure full-time places? It would seem useful to
examine, with a view to wider application, this question of
competition for entry to full-time higher education and the
lifetime career patterns of those who follow conventional
higher education courses, part-time and correspondence
instruction and those who decide not to undergo higher
education at all.

In Western Europe, the issue is made more difficult
because of the widely held belief that the provision of
higher education should be based mainly on the individual
demand for places. Not that this has by any means been
universally applied. In the United Kingdom the rate at
which science and non-science places have been created in
universities has been influenced by perceived manpower needs
and the provision of places in medical schools and teacher
training colleges has always been linked closely to
estimates of the needs for doctors and teachers. In France
the Grandes Ecoles have never been expanded to take account
of the enormous individual demand for places at these
institutions and in Sweden it appears likely that provision
of university places will henceforward be linked more
closely to estimated manpower needs. However, the fact
remains that a high proportion of the places in higher
education in most Western European countries are there
because it is believed that students and their parents want
them rather than because of any specific idea of labour
market demands for qualified manpower. These places are
provided free or on a very highly subsidised basis. In many
countries, not only the higher education itself but also a
substantial part of the maintenance of students is provided
free, thus reducing considerably the costs of higher
education to the individual in terms of income foregone.
The demand for higher education by individuals is not,
therefore, a true "demand" in the economic sense of a desire

for the satisfaction of which a price is offered. Rather,
it is a claim for a free good the right to which is offered
to all who achieve some previous level of educational
attainment.[1] Even if, as has been suggested in this report,
the free good is essentially a lottery ticket which carries
only a probability of substantial rewards in terms of career
advancement, the fact that it is free, or offered at a very
low price in relation to the rewards to which it gives the
chance of access, ensures a high demand for it. As is the
case with all gambling operations, the market abounds in
myths and half-truths. There are also severe information
lags - children may be given information that was relevant
when their parents or teachers were concerned with higher
education.

In these countries, the most pressing need is for
more, and more reliable, information about current
education/labour market relations. In only a very few of
them is any reliable statistical information collected
regularly on employment by educational qualifications, on
the experience of new school leavers and graduates in
finding their first employment and on the earnings of
workers with different educational qualifications. If the
problem of the employment of qualified manpower is
considered a serious issue, this information must be
regularly collected and carefully analysed.

Until it is available, any analysis of
education/labour market relationships must remain highly
speculative and policy recommendations tentative. However,
on the assumption that the main lines of the analysis of
this report will prove to be valid, a number of fairly clear
pointers do emerge.

First, and perhaps easiest, the informational links
between the educational system and the labour market must be
strengthened. What this means in practice is that there
should be national systems of student counselling and
guidance and that advice services must be grounded in a
thorough knowledge of the real and prospective states of the
labour market. Furthermore, these services should carry
enough weight not only to influence students in deciding
whether to take particular educational courses but also to
influence the courses that are provided.

One feature of higher education in Eastern Europe that
might be adopted in some form in other countries is the
obligation on employers actually to take on the graduates
they have claimed to require in their manpower plans. This

----

[1] In some countries, this creates further distortions in
that since secondary education is not so generously
subsidised as higher education, some richer parents are
willing to pay for private education in order to ensure that
their children get free tickets for higher education.

is already seen to some extent in the scholarships provided by the armed services and many large firms. There is a case for extending this approach, particularly at the upper levels of higher education such as postgraduate study. It need not preclude places being provided for students who do not wish to commit themselves to enter a specific employment, but they would be aware of the risks they were taking.[1]

The establishment of such links between education and employment combined with adequate student counselling services can do much to avoid one of the most pervasive reasons for graduate unemployment. As has been shown, most unemployed graduates are those who have not yet entered the labour force. They prefer to indulge in a perfectly rational search activity so as to ensure that in taking one job they are not foregoing opportunities of higher pay or better career prospects somewhere else. Counselling services help students to undertake these search activities while they are still undergoing their higher education rather than subsequently.

But while counselling services can do much to dispel the fog which currently surrounds education/labour market relationships, they can do little to overcome the basic problem if it is true that the current subsidy, tax and salary situation results in it being rational for individuals to accept a given probability of unemployment in return for a given probability of a high return.

In order to deal with this fundamental problem, a radical change in the criteria underlying the provision of higher education is required. There are two possibilities; one is the planned economy solution already described in which the number of places in higher education is limited to the number of places it is believed the labour market can absorb, the allocation of these places being based essentially on a system of rationing in which points are awarded for academic performance, work experience and various other criteria. Minor maladjustments resulting from incorrect forecasting can be overcome by arrangements for late entry and part-time higher education. The market economy solution would be to create institutional arrangements which ensure that the private costs of higher education more nearly reflect the true social costs. This would in effect raise the price of "lottery tickets" so that students would consider carefully whether they were still worth buying when the probability of loss through unemployment reached high levels. Possible discrimination

----

[1] It should, however, be noted that in the United Kingdom the reorganisation of teacher training outlined in the Government's White Paper, _Education:___A__framework__for expansion_, December 1972, will loosen the ties between colleges of education and subsequent employment as teachers.

against children from poor families who cannot afford to pay
the costs could be circumvented by the establishment of what
are known as income-contingent loan schemes. This means
that students would be given loans in order to finance their
higher education but that they would make repayments only
when their incomes exceeded a certain level. However, if
the repayment of loans is income-contingent, the risk of
unemployment ceases to be a deterrent to students, because
while they are unemployed any debt repayments due are
remitted.[1]

The effect of loans in curbing higher education
expansion when the labour market moves against graduates is
shown by the case of Sweden, where there has been a sharp
fall in enrolments in recent years which can partly be
attributed to the unwillingness of young people to incur
substantial debts in the face of an increasing risk that no
substantial economic benefits may ensue.

The financing of higher education via student loans
may have another advantage in helping to curb graduate
unemployment. If a larger share of their income were
received from student fees, higher education establishments
might well become more responsive to the needs of students
instead of being guided entirely by the academic ethos. To
the extent that students wished to apply labour market
criteria in making their educational choices, they would
help to steer universities and other institutions in this
direction.

Finally, it can perhaps be repeated that to some
extent, graduate unemployment is an aspect of general
unemployment and although it has some special features which
necessitate special treatment, none of the measures
suggested for dealing with it can be entirely successful in
an economy which is not already economically healthy.

However, even in a situation of general full
employment, the problem of excessive expansion of higher
education may remain in that, although the possession of an
educational qualification becomes less and less of an
advantage, its absence is more and more of a disadvantage.
In the past the scarcity of educational qualifications meant
that the possession of one was a sufficient but not
necessary condition for career success. A situation is now
emerging in which a degree is a necessary but not a
sufficient condition for a successful career.

----

[1] This is not to deny that loans have other
justifications besides their deterrent effects. In fact
most protagonists of loans would deny that the aim is to
deter students; they propose them on equity grounds since,
in general, graduates earn higher salaries than non-
graduates.

If employers persist in using the possession of
educational qualifications as an indication of ability - or
more important their absence as an indication of lack of
ability - the final responsibility for adjustment must lie
with the labour market and must be achieved through flexible
salary policies and the encouragement of occupational
mobility through the widespread development of retraining
schemes, recurrent education and other ways of enabling the
labour force to respond to changing economic circumstances.

CHAPTER IV

MIGRATION OF WORKERS AS AN ELEMENT IN EMPLOYMENT POLICY

WESTERN EUROPE

International economic migrations[1] are caused by unequal economic development. Fifty or one hundred years ago, this meant that migrations had their origin in the process of industrialisation. At that time, the main movements in Europe were from East to West and to overseas countries. Present day migrations, which are mainly from Southern to Western Europe - from developing to highly industrialised countries - find their origin in the transition of Western Europe's industrialised countries to "post-industrial" societies.[2]

Rising expectations fuelled by extended education and the mass media as well as a favourable labour market situation have led, as has been noted earlier in this report, to the growing aversion of large sections of Western Europe's workers to heavy, dirty, dangerous or unpleasant low-pay and low-status jobs and latterly also to jobs involving monotonous assembly-type work or inconvenient working hours; these kinds of jobs are classified together here under the term "socially undesirable jobs". Foreign workers have been engaged to fill the vacancies.[3]

The fact that over time some foreigners, particularly the better educated, filter through into well-paid and respected jobs does not alter the fact that most contemporary economic migrations are into socially undesirable jobs. It should also be noted that, while the small volume of movement of high-level personnel between Europe's industrialised countries does not give rise to any concern about a "brain-drain", there are a few "brain-drain" streams from developing to industrialised countries both
----

[1] The terms migration/immigration/emigration and migrant/immigrant/emigrant do not imply any judgment what-soever on the de jure or de facto status of migratory movements in Europe.

[2] Cf. W.R. Böhning: The economic effects of the employment of foreign workers: with special reference to the labour markets of Western Europe's post-industrial countries (OECD, Paris: MS/M/404/415, 1972), esp. Ch. II.

[3] See also S. Castles and G. Kosack: Immigrant workers and class structure in Western Europe (London, Oxford University Press, 1973).

within Europe and from outside into Europe which cannot be disregarded. For example, there are large numbers of doctors in the United Kingdom from the Indian sub-continent and of Yugoslav and Turkish doctors as well as teachers in the Federal Republic of Germany. Not all educated migrants work in positions commensurate with their training - many, in fact, can be found in what have been termed socially undesirable jobs.

What in the 1950s looked like a transitory labour shortage turned out to be a long-term structural maladjustment of the labour market and Western European countries have allowed themselves to become dependent upon the continuing import of foreign labour for the functioning of crucial sectors of the economy and the maintenance of their living standards.

Table 9 in the Appendix gives an indication of the size, origin and growth of the foreign work force in Western Europe's main immigration countries. The figures refer to officially registered or counted workers of foreign nationalities and also where applicable to immigrants who hold the citizenship of the receiving country but originate from territories formerly administered by that receiving country. The figures do not include naturalised foreigners or illegal immigrants. Even the official registers and census counts tend to underenumerate the number of foreigners actually present.

The Austrian "quota" data, for instance, are estimated to be about 20 per cent below the real number of foreign workers (incidentally, the "quota" figures crossed the 200,000 mark in August 1972 and the trend was still upwards). The French and British censuses are known to have undercounted by 15 per cent or more nationalities where single male households or multi-occupied dwellings predominated. The French figures for 1970 in the table are the least complete; the difference between the employee figures and reliable estimates of Portuguese and North African resident foreigners in 1970 in particular[1] is inconsistent with the known high degree of labour force participation by these groups and their low degree of family reunion. France, of course, is particularly affected by partly illegal and partly spontaneous migrations, which are later "regularised". The French censuses also reveal that an average of 10 per cent of the foreign labour force is self-employed. It is likely, therefore, that the true figure for France at the beginning of the 1970s is nearer 2 million than 1.5 million.

----

[1] See Hommes et migrations - documents, No. 808 of 1 June 1971. The number of Portuguese residents is given as 600,000.

In the enlarged European Communities (EC) alone, there
are currently well over 6 million immigrant workers.[1] To
these can be added almost 1.5 million in Austria, Norway,
Sweden and Switzerland. In countries North of the Alps,
there are therefore more immigrant workers than there are
indigenous employees in Austria, Belgium, Denmark and
Ireland taken together.

Furthermore, even the traditional labour-sending
countries in the Mediterranean area have begun to employ
foreigners on a significant scale. The table puts Italy's
officially registered foreign workers at 40,000 (and it
seems that these are no longer, as they were in the past
mainly white-collar workers in commerce). Additionally,
several thousand Tunisians have recently arrived in Sicily
more or less illegally to take up some of the worst-paid
jobs there. Spain is estimated to have 100,000 foreign
workers in its borders, about two-fifths of these being
Moroccans and Algerians, many of whom immigrated illegally.[2]
Portuguese workers who have been refused entry into France
also sometimes end up working in Spain. In Greece, about
30,000 Egyptians, Sudanese, Ethiopians and Somalis have been
stated to be working in certain industries, such as mining,
hotels and catering. Yugoslavia has filled some of the gaps
left by its emigrants with workers from Italy. Even Finland
is already considering the need to import workers.

In the case of the Mediterranean countries, the
employment of foreigners is only in part related to the
process of industrialisation. To some degree, it is
emigration-induced in the sense that the familiarisation of
emigrant workers with the wages and working conditions north
of the Alps often leads to their refusing to undertake
certain kinds of work on their return, an attitude which
tends to be transmitted to the non-migrant population.

Finally, a word is in order here about the statistical
shortcomings in both receiving and sending countries. These
are highly regrettable in view of the long history of
migration in Europe and its economic and political
importance; it is serious when countries which strive to
have a policy of immigration or emigration are unable to
monitor the effects of their measures; moreover, there is
no possibility of conducting informed public debate about
----

[1] Luxembourg, which is not included in table 9, also
employs about 35,000 foreign workers, mainly Italians. The
Netherlands figures for 1972 exclude all foreigners who have
been employed there for over five years, thus presumably the
majority of the true total is covered but by no means the
great majority.

[2] At the end of April 1973, it was reported that 15,000
Moroccans had arrived in Barcelona in five days to work in
the building industry.

the goals and means of migration policies if the indicators are lacking.

Recent research on West European migration statistics undertaken by the Council of Europe has fortunately led to constructive proposals and it is recommended that the countries concerned should observe the principles laid down in the Council's Resolution (72)18 on "Methods of compiling statistics on international migration of workers" adopted by the Committee of Ministers on 30 May 1972.

Migration and the labour market of receiving countries

Apart from France, where immigration policy was originally demographically motivated, West European countries started their recruitment of foreigners with the intention of plugging labour market gaps with workers who were not expected to cause a significant or sustained pressure on the infrastructure, namely single workers or married workers without their dependants, who would return home if and when the labour shortage disappeared. Neither family reunion nor settlement was envisaged (except perhaps in Sweden).

The premises of this approach were firstly, that a high rate of economic growth should not be held up in one country for lack of labour so long as there was a labour surplus in neighbouring countries. This found international expression in the OEEC (subsequently OECD) Decision of October 1953, which provided that applications by employers to employ foreign workers who were nationals of signatory countries should be granted virtually automatically if national workers were not immediately available, provided wages and working conditions corresponded to those prevailing for nationals in similar work and provided that the employment of these foreign workers would not endanger industrial peace (Decision of the Council C(53)251 (Final)).[1]

Secondly, the approach assumed that to fill given vacancies with available foreigners would dispose of the unfilled labour demand in the economy and that developments in the sending and the receiving countries would reduce the
----

[1] It should be added that as early as 1964, the OECD reconsidered the premises on which the 1953 Decision had been based, partly because of the new developments in the EEC. It was felt, however, that instead of amending the Decision it would be more useful to undertake regular examinations ("confrontations") of migration policies in the Working Party on Migration which, in addition, launched a valuable programme of research.

need to employ foreign workers or even dispose of it altogether.

Thirdly, the approach assumed that there were enough eligible workers in neighbouring countries who would conform to the expected behaviour; in particular, it assumed that the time horizon of eligible migrants would coincide with the interests of the receiving country and that these migrants could be kept to a short-term horison through legal sanctions.

The following examination will show that the first premise needs revision because the others have turned out to be only partially true.

Migrants' motivations and characteristics

The time horizon. Apart from seasonal migrants, there are undoubtedly many migrants with a short-term return migration goal, but the largest single group has no definite time horison whatsoever.[1] Their primary concern is to earn as much money as possible as quickly as possible. To achieve this, they take any job offered, hoping to change to a better one in due course.

The job, however, puts the migrant at the bottom of the wage and status hierarchy. This is in part due to his pre-migration traits - lack of education, different language, etc. - and in part to the migration control system, which in extreme cases leads to the engagement of foreign graduates as dustmen or bricklayers, for example. This is one reason why even with overtime, shift work or moon lighting, the migrant has to adjust his time horizon quite quickly. Another is the high cost of living - a consideration which eludes the typical migrant before departure. Sooner or later, even the shortest time horizon needs to be extended if the migrant is not to admit failure to himself, his wife or extended family. Available data confirm that, regardless of nationality and background, in all migrant populations those who extend their originally short-term intentions are far more numerous than those who keep to them or curtail them.[2]

Once a migrant has been enmeshed in the temptations and rewards of the consumer society and once the prospect of

----

[1] See for instance Rudolf Braun: Sozio-kulturelle Probleme der Eingliederung italienischer Arbeitskräfte in der Schweiz (Erlenback-Zürich: Eugen Rentsch Verlag, 1970), and Stadt Ludwigshafen, Amt für Grundlagenforschung und Stadtentwicklung: Bericht über die Lage der Gastarbeiter in Ludwigshafen am Rhein, by Harald Kühne (1971).

[2] Cf. for instance R. Braun, op. cit., pp. 79, 473 and 488, and OECD, op. cit., Ch. IIb.

finding more stable employment and higher real wages than in
the home country has been demonstrated, the psychological
costs of separation from his home weigh less and less
relative to the material gains obtained. Thus the short-
term migrant slowly turns into a long-term emigrant.

This increasing duration of stay in the country of
immigration goes hand in hand with decreasing acceptance of
the living conditions accorded him there, which are those of
a subproletariat. The manifest achievement of a higher
standard of living by workers of the host country impels the
migrant to strive for the same better conditions. And he is
quite prepared to pay for it (quite apart from the fact that
migrants tend to pay more for the same or worse services
than the host population). The often-heard argument that
migrants do not want to live in better surroundings because
of their desire to save is a generalisation which is refuted
by empirical evidence.[1]

Marital status. The changing time horizon should be
seen in conjunction with the fact that migration streams do
not exclusively consist of young, single, male workers. On
the contrary, some of the original migration streams in
post-war Europe contained mostly female workers (for
resident domestic service and the hotel and catering
industries in Switzerland for example, and the same holds
true in Great Britain today). Many of these women were
married. More important is the fact that there is no
inexhaustible surplus of young, single, male workers from
any one sending country and that, even though some social
factors may favour this group initially, other social
factors soon redress the balance and induce married males to
come forward and to seek the reunion of their families after
a short while abroad.[2]

It is in fact the married male worker who accounts for
the increasing length of stay, whether living unaccompanied
or tending to settle after having been joined by his wife
and possibly his children.[3] Staying on means that the
institutionally enforced separation finally begins to break

---

[1] See, for example, Ernst Zieris: Wohnverhältnisse von
Familien ausländischer Arbeitnehmer in Nordrhein-Westfalen,
Auswertung einer Erhebung des Ministeriums für Arbeit,
Gesundheit und Soziales des Landes Nordrhein-Westfalen
(Düsseldorf: Kurt Dehl, 1971), p. 62 f., and Stadt
Ludwigshafen, op. cit., p. 26.

[2] Cf. OECD, op. cit., Ch. IIb.

[3] After a migration has been under way for a few years,
as many as half the single foreigners employed in a
receiving country may be related to immigrant families
settling there. These people will also tend to settle
rather than conform to the picture of a single worker
emigrating temporarily.

down unless receiving countries are prepared to pursue a
policy of requiring every married worker to leave the
country before he becomes eligible for family reunion.
Family reunion leads to settlement in the great majority of
cases. Thus new immigration streams sooner or later come to
resemble non-migrant populations in terms of marital status,
at least as far as the male side is concerned. Just as 60-
70 per cent of male national workers in receiving countries
are married, so are 60-70 per cent of the male immigrant
workers. The only difference is that many of the latter are
separated from their wives and children, most of all where
the migration is of relatively recent origin and where the
receiving country pursues a policy of preventing family
reunion.

Employment of women. A further consequence of this
development is that, in course of time, women tend to form
an increasing proportion of the immigrant population, be it
as workers (because this is one way to reunite families) or
as inactive dependants (if and when the criteria for family
reunion are fulfilled).

Married women workers may even be the original cause
of family reunion. Although the entry of women into
resident domestic service or the hotel and catering industry
is sometimes confined to single women, manufacturing
employers seldom impose, or are seldom willing to accept
such a restriction, and foreign women workers in
manufacturing quickly exceed the numbers in domestic service
or hotel and catering. In fact, the employment of foreign
women is fairly popular with West European employers in some
kinds of precision work, the electrical and optical
industries for example, or in traditionally low-wage
industries such as textiles and clothing, food, drink and
tobacco.

There is one further feature of the employment of
foreign women which it is imperative to note, namely their
large-scale employment in hospital services, especially as
nurses and ancillary workers. In some countries, a large
proportion of these are of non-European origin. One cannot
but "question the values of a society which attaches so
little standing, in terms of income and status, to some of
its most important functions that the indigenous population
avoids them wherever it can; one (must) also question the
blatant contradiction between social priority and actual
social status in the case of, for example, nurses, on the
one hand, and secretaries, on the other."[1]

The demand for additional infrastructure. The
interplay of increasing duration of stay and family reunion

----

[1] W.R. Böhning: The migration of workers in the United
Kingdom and the European Community (London, Oxford University Press, 1972), p. 145.

produces an immigrant population which is permanent in its presence even though only parts of it may intend to settle for good. A permanent population with partly rotating membership entails significant demands on the existing infrastructure. On average, these demands may not be as great as those of an indigenous stationary population of the same size, but the fact that they are scarcely met does not mean that they are not there. Every addition to the work force and population requires a commensurate addition to the infrastructure.

Immigrant populations are usually concentrated in the highly industrialised areas of Western Europe and particularly in the great conurbations. Within the conurbations there is a continuing concentration in inner city areas vacated by the indigenous worker's move to suburbia. The concentration continues even in cases where the inflow of migrants from abroad has been severely restricted, as in Great Britain and Switzerland.

More specifically, the social chain of causation runs from immigration into low-paid jobs to ghetto-like housing[1] to reduced chances of adequate schooling to the formation of prejudices of a class, ethnic or racial character. Governments have rightly become concerned about the social problems turning up in the wake of migration.[2] But they have not yet seriously faced up to the fact that only a radical improvement will prevent the emergence of the subproletariat of tomorrow within their own cities.

One consequence of repeated talk about the "problems" connected with immigration is that it pulls the carpet from under the avowed policies of equal treatment and "integration". To talk about migrants as if they caused problems and thereby to label them as a problem group inevitably encourages hostility to them. This runs counter to the basic requirements of a policy of equal treatment in law and in practice.

Is it necessary to mention here that in the receiving countries there are increasing numbers of influential persons and groups acutely aware of the often appalling

----

[1] Be it in socially isolating hostels, decaying inner cities or the outlying bidonvilles.

[2] This is not to say that migrant workers are a prime cause of social problems, though hardly any government has said this as clearly as the British Government recently when the Home Secretary stated that "it is essential to realise that in many cases we should be suffering from exactly the same problems of social tension, conflict and crime if the old white population had remained in these areas and immigrants had never moved in". Quoted in Runnymede Trust Bulletin, No. 42 (April 1973).

living conditions of foreign workers who are opposed to the
concept of using them as a rotating labour force. What
nobody thought of questioning in 1900 or 1930, what nobody
questioned in 1954 had become questionable in 1964 and is
resented and fought against in 1974. In affluent societies,
one expects governments to help their most disadvantaged
strata. Western Europe can afford this financially, and in
its own conscience it cannot afford not to help. It cannot
be in the public interest to have a discontented
subproletariat with rotating membership filling up the
decaying inner cities.

Last but not least, the non-discrimination requirement
of the European Communities extends with supranational force
to about one-third of all foreign workers in Community
countries. But the Commission of the Communities has long
realised the anomaly of discriminating between Italians and,
say, Spaniards for no other reason than their nationality.
It has therefore proposed that "the benefits enjoyed by
Community workers will have to be extended by stages to the
whole Community's immigrant labour force, starting with
workers from associated countries ...".[1] This means that not
only one out of three foreign workers in Western Europe, but
before long one out of two and possibly eight out of ten
will be entitled to freedom from institutional
discrimination. Considering the standard-setting influence
of the Community, the remaining receiving countries - mainly
Sweden, Switzerland and Austria - are likely to have to
adjust their immigration systems too (Sweden, of course, is
in many ways a pace-setter already).

It should be added that, consequent upon resolutions
adopted by the 1971 and 1972 International Labour
Conferences, the ILO is considering the need for various
complementary instruments relating to the situation of
migrant workers. These would cover their housing situation,
social services in the widest sense, as well as the problem
of family reunion.[2]

Employment effects

The demand for foreign workers originates in decisions
by private employers and, to a lesser degree, public

----

[1] Commission of the European Communities: Preliminary
guidelines for a social policy programme in the Community
(17 March 1971), Supplement 2/71 to No. 4/71 Bulletin of the
European Communities. This proposal is retained in the new
Guidelines for the Social Action Programme of April 1973 in
which, moreover, a co-ordination of immigration policies
towards third countries by 31 December 1974 is proposed.

[2] See ILO: Migrant workers, Report VII(1), International Labour Conference, 59th Session, 1974.

authorities. In responding to employers' requests, governments have enabled these micro-economic demands for labour to be met, but have unwittingly introduced new problems on the macro-economic plane.

There are two reasons for this. Firstly, the infrastructural repercussions of immigrant populations; and secondly, but probably less important, the effects of the employment of foreigners on production and competitiveness.

Infrastructural effects. Recent research has shown[1] that a given labour shortage produces a new labour shortage if one tries to satisfy it with a migrant population of typical marital composition while making commensurate social capital provision. The actual vacancies are of course filled with imported labour, but new ones arise through multifarious charges on the housing and service sector.

The economies feed on migrants and migrants feed on the economies. There is no end to it. At the beginning of the seventies, the Federal Republic of Germany, for example, admitted 1,000 times as many immigrants per annum as the United States adjusted for the size and population of this traditional country of immigration. This figure would merely be halved if related solely to permanent settlement.

It is not surprising, therefore, that governments have recently come to doubt the macro-economic utility and validity of employers' demands for foreign workers. The Bavarian Minister of the Interior stated unequivocally: "The admittance of foreign employees for a stay in the Federal Republic of Germany should in the future not be allowed to be ruled primarily by the real or presumed demand for labour of individual employers. Rather the multi-dimensional public interests, ranging from the infrastructure to environmental pollution, must be given a decisive weight."[2]

General economic effects. The fact that macro-economically the satisfaction of labour demand is to some extent illusory does not mean, however, that the receiving countries do not reap tangible benefits from labour import, especially in the short term. First of all, the constant satisfaction of given demand, particularly in bottleneck situations, permits smoother running of the economy at higher growth rates. The external turnover of the foreign work force imparts a disproportionately large degree of flexibility to the labour market.

----

[1] Cf. Centraal Planbureau: Economische effecten voor Nederland van de werving van buitenlandse werknemers (The Hague, March 1972), and OECD, op. cit., Ch. IIa.

[2] From a memorandum of the Bayerische Staatsministerium des Innern to the Koordinierungskreis ausländischer Arbeitnehmer, Bonn, 1972.

This basic effect is, however, subject to decreasing mobility deriving from increasing length of stay and the degree to which governments seek to dampen down the inflow of additional workers or are unable to enforce the principle of rotation. Migrants who are long-term stayers tend to resemble comparable indigenous groups in their mobility behaviour. Policies which implicitly or explicitly further the permanent settlement of migrants therefore decrease this economic benefit (although they may have other important benefits). To offset this, a greater absolute number of mobile workers would be needed in order, ceteris paribus, to achieve a given flexibility effect.

In contemporary immigration, the problem with wages is not so much one of "cheap labour" as it was at the beginning of this century. Trade unions are generally able to see that the worst excesses are avoided, although one should not be complacent about the occasional reports of sweated labour which come to light, especially where migrants enter outside the normal channels of recruitment or are hired out by subcontractors.[1] Today, however, the problem lies rather more in the hardening of wage differentials between socially undesirable jobs and others.

Foreign workers' remittances to their home countries have a deflationary impact, but the net effect is probably much lower than is generally assumed. Money sent across the exchanges returns in one form or another, possibly in the form of export demand. This problem will be returned to in the next section.

Wherever foreigners are employed in export industries - and this holds true throughout Western Europe - the terms of trade of the exporting country are likely to benefit through the dampening of factor price and goods price inflation. The immigration-induced relief of wage pressure obtains predominantly in manufacturing industries (while being offset in the aggregate by induced pressure in construction and services). If one relates the improved terms of trade to the improved prospects of selling abroad brought about by the flow of remittances, one cannot escape the conclusion that the importation of labour widens the competitive gap between sending and receiving countries and generates employment in the latter. The sending country, on the other hand, labours under a handicap derived from its own emigration. Without countervailing forces, emigration-induced unemployment occurs. As far as the receiving country is concerned, "it would not be too far from the truth to say that parts of the export sector import both raw material and labour, export the finished product to the

---

[1] Cf. the description by S. Castle and G. Kosack of the situation in France in Immigrant workers and class structure, op. cit.

countries of origin and keep the profits to themselves".[1]
Obviously, here is a situation of interdependence and strain
which calls for an international solution, for example by
bringing the work to the worker instead of the other way
round.

The negative effect of labour immigration on the
receiving country's productivity has been considered by many
economists to be of crucial importance. However, the
anticipated adverse effect on productivity seems in reality
not to have taken place or to have been overtaken by
immigrant-induced productivity growth.[2] The heated debate on
capital deepening versus capital widening should not be
lightly dismissed, although it has perhaps been somewhat
unreal and shortsighted in that the question at issue is
rather the type of technology that is maintained by the
availability of foreign labour, namely the technology of
semi-automation: continuous production processes requiring
mechanical repetitive tasks without any skill content. Jobs
in this category, especially when they are badly paid and
involve shift work, form part of what have been called
socially undesirable jobs.

Finally, as far as the social capital requirements of
migrant worker populations are concerned, their age
composition, their lower dependency ratio, and their high
external turnover burden the receiving countries with
objectively lower social capital requirements than a
comparable number of indigenous workers. Long-term
settlement diminishes this favourable effect only very
slowly. On the other hand, migrant workers contribute to
public receipts in proportion to their numbers. This
contrasts sharply with the reluctance of public authorities
to cater for the immigrant-induced pressure on the
infrastructure. The net result is a highly favourable
effect on the receiving countries' finances and a highly
unfavourable effect on the living conditions of migrants.

In conclusion it might be said that migrant workers
have not only contributed to the maintenance or expansion of
production and services but have also induced additional
employment through the smooth running of the economy in
general and the favourable effect on competitiveness in
particular.

The extension of the recruitment areas

The "self-feeding" character of contemporary
migrations has meant that ever larger numbers and new
sending countries have become involved. Even geographically

----

[1] OECD, op. cit., p. 65.

[2] Ibid., Ch. IIId.

and culturally distant countries in Africa, Asia, Latin
America and the Caribbean (mainly former colonial
territories) have sent migrants, thereby weakening the
connection between vicinity and likelihood of return, as
well as highlighting the social problems.

The development in the original European Communities
exemplifies the trends at work. At the time of the creation
of the European Communities, about two-thirds of the total
labour immigration originated in member States. Today, this
proportion stands at one-fifth (the absolute number of
intra-EC migrations has increased considerably but has now
become stable). This was to some degree the result of the
relatively stagnant supply from Italy. New sources were
tapped in Turkey and Yugoslavia, which proved abundant.
Yugoslavia fitted the bill because it was to some extent
still a developing country with labour surpluses in
agriculture, because its economic reforms in the mid-sixties
had set free a large number of workers which it was unable
to re-employ immediately, and because it was not averse to
seeing some of its labour surplus emigrating, at least
temporarily, and remitting large sums of money. Turkey's
background as a country with large labour surpluses and
trade deficits destined it to become a country of
emigration, even though historically it had not been one.

Towards the end of the sixties, some countries which
had hitherto drawn their foreign workers only from Europe
extended the areas of origin to non-European countries,
especially North Africa. Latin America and Asia also came
into consideration as potential supplying regions. But
while the Federal Republic of Germany and the Netherlands,
for example, concluded recruitment agreements with Morocco
and Tunisia, France already began to tighten up its
migration control over Algerians. More recently, France has
begun to reconsider its migration links with its former
colonies in sub-Saharan Africa, and the same holds true for
the Netherlands as regards Surinam and the Netherlands
Antilles. The United Kingdom controlled free immigration
from India, Pakistan, the West Indies and Africa as early as
1962. The total number of voucher holders immigrating from
the "New Commonwealth" (but excluding United Kingdom
passport holders from East Africa) declined from 28,700 in
1963 to 4,700 in 1967 and 1,300 in 1972. Increasing concern
over the never ending supply-demand spiral has recently led
the Federal Republic of Germany to consider that a
stabilisation of the present annual intake of foreign
workers might well be achieved with the available supply in,
primarily, Yugoslavia and Turkey, provided the principle of
rotation is not enforced too rigidly.

Thus the seemingly inevitable extension of the area of
labour origin to more and more non-European countries
appears to have been halted, if not reversed. This should
be seen in relation to projected labour surpluses, not only

in Yugoslavia and Turkey[1], but elsewhere. The present
receiving countries of Western Europe, with the possible
exception of the United Kingdom, will continue to be short
of labour.[2] This shortage will be the more pronounced the
less assimilative the policies of the receiving countries.
While qualitative and social factors may gain in importance
relative to quantitative economic considerations, there is,
given current economic and technological trends, no
foreseeable end to continued labour immigration in Western
Europe.

Mere restriction - a false alternative

The tendency of contemporary economic migration to
feed on itself and the undeniable social problems arising in
the wake of immigration have resulted in a tendency towards
more restrictive policies throughout Western Europe. Yet
restriction does not solve any of the fundamental problems,
for the simple reason that it does not touch their cause.

Restrictive policies without accompanying measures
leave the problem of socially undesirable jobs unresolved.
Moreover, they may lead to economic distortions and deplete
essential services of necessary manpower (hospitals,
transport, post, etc.). A selective restriction policy is
administratively feasible under present conditions of
migration control and it may be useful to apply such a
policy now to ensure the staffing of essential public
services, bearing in mind that in a few years about half the
immigrant labour force may enjoy freedom of movement inside
the countries of Western Europe.

----

[1] See Luisa Danieli: "Labour scarcities and labour
redundancies in Europe by 1980: An experimental study", in
M. Livi Bacci, ed., The demographic and social pattern of
emigration from the Southern European Countries
(Publicazioni del Dipartimento Statistico-Matematico
dell'Universita di Firenze, 1972), table 7, p. 159.

[2] Ibid., table 5, p. 152. For a more up-to-date
evaluation, see W.R. Böhning: The migration of workers, op.
cit., ch. 7. With hindsight one can see that L. Danieli's
projections for the United Kingdom are wide of the mark
because her trend analysis is based on the favourable labour
market situation of the fifties and first half of the
sixties. Since 1966-67, the United Kingdom's situation has
changed for both economic and social reasons. In a recent
debate on immigration, the Government's confidence was
expressed repeatedly that in future the country would be
able to maintain its economy "without steadily increasing
numbers of immigrant unskilled labour brought in from
abroad". House of Commons, Official report, 22 November
1972, col. 1359.

Restrictive policies, moreover, leave the social problems unresolved. They may embitter the immigrant population and worsen host-migrant relations without even satisfying the xenophobic demands they are sometimes intended to pacify. And restrictions - like talk of the problems which immigrants "cause" - are the opposite of what is required for an effective policy of equality of treatment in the receiving countries. One cannot imply, on the one hand, that immigrants are undesirable and, on the other, expect the host population and its administrators not to discriminate against them.

Furthermore, restrictive policies are not solely a unilateral affair. They may hurt sending countries as well as other receiving countries and sour the relations between them. Thus, the analysis of labour migration into receiving countries points out the need for close international co-operation.

Countries will certainly be able to reap significant economic benefits from continued labour imports by relying on the principle of voluntary rotation. But some of the extreme models of forced rotation put forward for discussion are not only unworthy of democratic and affluent societies, they come close to treating labour as a commodity; and they run counter to the principle embodied in the Migration for Employment Recommendation (Revised), 1949 (No. 86) that "in countries in which the employment of migrants is subject to restrictions, these restrictions should as far as possible cease to be applied to migrants who have regularly resided in the country for a period, the length of which should not, as a rule, exceed five years." (Paragraph 16(2).)

Employment and social effects of migration in sending countries

Even though some European sending countries are, as indicated, on the verge of becoming labour-importing countries, their main preoccupation in the next five to ten years will be with their traditional emigration problems, such as attempting to ensure that emigration relieves unemployment in the regions of the country where it is most serious, that emigrants' remittances help to solve national balance of payments problems, that emigrants enjoy certain minimum conditions of work and life in the countries in which they are employed, and that a proportion of them return home with skills useful to the development of the home country. A brief survey will show that these countries, too, have reason to doubt the wisdom of their past policies.

First of all, emigration is supposed to relieve a country's unemployment. To some degree, this is no doubt

what happens; but it is neither sufficient in itself nor as
unequivocal as appears at first sight. Receiving countries
are naturally interested in engaging only the best workers
available.   This entails a "skimming off" effect which (to
put it in a negative way) may not always touch the hard-core
unemployed. In fact, it is often the better educated and
more skilled worker who comes forward for emigration and
sometimes even the man on whom the employment of others
depends.   As long as sending countries are unable or
unwilling to control their emigrants tightly (not to
prohibit emigration, for this would conflict with the
Universal Declaration of Human Rights), they lose not only
the more employable of the unemployed but also workers in
relatively good and important industrial or agricultural
jobs who are sometimes difficult to replace. Thus it is by
no means clear that for every emigrant who was employed
there will be a corresponding reduction in unemployment or
underemployment.

Furthermore, any emigration entails a loss in
expenditure which, if sufficiently large in a given region,
could have a detrimental effect on the level of employment
there.   In the case of temporary international migration,
the loss of expenditure is potentially made good by
remittances. But considering that far from all migrants are
temporary, that at most one-third of their wages are
remitted and that an unknown but significant proportion of
this income is spent on consumer goods produced abroad, it
is far from certain that the net effect is positive in all
cases.

The sending countries have mainly been concerned with
remittances, particularly the closing of the trade deficit
and the use of the foreign currency so acquired for
investment in productive capacity.   The volume of
remittances has indeed reached enormous proportions. "The
current annual flow of remittances from all migrants in
Europe to their home countries is over $2.5 billion, which
is, as a comparison, well in excess of the total value of
actual lending disbursed world wide by the World Bank Group
each year."[1]

However, mechanically adding remittances to the trade
deficit makes even less sense than mechanically subtracting
emigrants from the unemployed, quite apart from the possibly
inflationary repercussions of such an inflow of disposable
income. On the individual level, remittances are used in
the first instance to cater for daily needs or to pay off
old debts.   A continuing inflow subsequently goes on
consumer goods, sometimes of quite a fancy kind and often of
foreign origin.   None of this expenditure is more than
marginally productive. Moreover, where the migrant extends
----

[1] I.M. Hume: "Migrant workers in Europe", Finance and
Development, Vol. 10, No. 1 (March 1973), p. 5.

his stay abroad and possibly sends for his family, the remittances begin to dry up.

In macro-economic terms, the foreign currency tends to be used, wherever there is no strict control of imports, to pay for imports of foreign consumer goods by the non-migrant population and by recipients of remittances. Thus there is an increasing familiarisation with foreign consumer goods brought about by the publicity surrounding migration and by the emigrants themselves. It leads in effect to a widespread disdain for domestic products and a higher value placed on foreign goods. And it leaves little if any room for domestic productive investment.

An empirical investigation for the Greek/Federal Republic of Germany exchanges showed that the familiarisation of Greek migrant workers and the Greek public at large with German goods led to a situation where the increasing volume of remittances covered a decreasing proportion of the growing trade deficit.[1] In other words, the net effect of emigrants' remittances appears to have been to worsen rather than improve the underlying balance of payments problem.

It is not intended to suggest here that remittances have no beneficial effect whatsoever. But attention needs to be drawn to the fact that they are something of a mixed blessing which requires closer governmental attention and channelling, and possibly an official campaign in favour of buying local goods.

Both sending and receiving countries have expressed the hope that temporary migration in Europe might help the former to acquire much needed skills through the return of workers from industrial countries. There are certainly individual cases where this holds true, but in over-all terms this is a forlorn hope. Intra-European migrants are not as transient as they are generally said to be. Moreover, it is principally the better educated and better qualified, the very manpower that is most needed in the sending countries, who tend to stay on. Those who return tend to be the least able to make the grade in the receiving country, and are hardly likely to be the type most needed in their countries of origin. The latter mainly need highly skilled and versatile manual workers, foremen and intermediate personnel[2] - not people who have "learnt" to empty dustbins in Munich, turn a screw at Renaults or wash dishes in Zurich.

----

[1] Marios Nikolinakos: "Zur Frage der Auswanderungseffekte in den Emigrationsländern", Das Argument, Vol. 13, No. 9/10 (December 1971), pp. 782-799.

[2] Cf. Madeleine Trebous: Migration and development: The case of Algeria (Paris, OECD Development Centre, 1970).

In actual fact the workers who do return, whatever their jobs were abroad and whatever their intentions are for the future, find it difficult to readjust to the conditions they once knew.[1] They feel that after what they have seen and experienced abroad they are entitled to something better back home. However, as it is difficult for the home country to provide either the same security of employment or high real wages and to provide better housing and living conditions (even though in relative terms these may be worse in the receiving country), they are likely to go abroad again and if indigenous workers are less and less willing to work for low wages in certain industries, the need to import labour from countries which have even lower wage levels becomes unavoidable.

A further worry is that, of the few who return permanently, too few envisage working in industrial jobs. Many prefer rather marginal jobs in service activities. This is a cultural phenomenon which requires a massive and sustained campaign by governments to popularise industrial employment, coupled perhaps with disincentives relating to the establishment of less productive activities in the tertiary sector.

Thus the main economic beenfits of emigration are far less certain than has been maintained hitherto. They may possibly be negative in the aggregate. On this account alone, sending countries need to keep their policies under close examination. There are a number of less important economic effects (such as the loss of expenditure invested in the upbringing of the migrant) which need not be considered here but which should perhaps form part of an over-all evaluation. There are also important non-economic considerations which should form part of an over-all evaluation but which cannot be considered here in detail - for example, the social repercussions in areas depopulated through emigration, with some women and children, the old and the senile left behind, the children often in a state of sadness, illness, fear and retarded mental development.

Socially the worst but most unlikely effect is that emigration breeds the emigrating subproletariat of tomorrow. Yugoslav teachers have reported[2] that pupils with parents abroad have little motivation to learn. "What does it

----

[1] See the reports on return movements to individual countries prepared by Messrs. I. Baucic, M. Poinard, N.J. Polizos and M. Roux and Mrs. N. Abadan for the OECD Working Party on Migration and summarised in B. Kayser: Cyclically-determined homeward flows of migrant workers (Paris, OECD, 1972).

[2] According to the Zagreb newspaper "VUS" quoted in Der Spiegel, No. 44/1972.

matter whether I am a good pupil. If not, I shall go and work in Germany" is a typical response. In the minds of these children, the prospect of unskilled work abroad is already more attractive than extended schooling, especially if the latter means prolonged separation from their parents. Some pupils leave school before the end of compulsory education, return home after a year or two with a camera or car and "infect" other pupils with the same desire.

Clearly, the sending countries do not profit as much from emigration as they expect and certainly less than the receiving countries. Hardly any of the problems they face can be solved in a unilateral way. If they resent the integrationist or assimilative policies of receiving countries because they want to see their workers return, they can do little more than protest. If they want to prevent the emigration of skilled workers or deter them through economic disincentives, they can achieve this only if receiving countries do not admit anybody except those presented to them by the sending countries. If they want to reabsorb returnants in an orderly way, they can do so only if receiving countries co-ordinate their policies with them.

Suggestions for action

There is an undeniable need for more co-ordination and co-operation between emigration and immigration countries. The enlargement of the European Communities, both through the entry of new members and the association of Mediterranean countries should impel governments to think in multilateral terms from the start rather than seeking a bilateral solution. If in the near future about half the foreign workers in the whole of Western Europe are to form part of an institutionalised common labour market, there is nothing to be gained by trying to solve problems bilaterally. For example, watertight migration control between two countries designed to prevent the emigration of skilled personnel is bound to fail if other European partners are not brought in the system. And unilateral action such as a sudden restrictive policy by a receiving country is bound to harm other receiving countries.

The single most important need, it is suggested, is to control the migration system more tightly. This does not go against the gradual extension of freedom of movement, for by migration system is meant the structures that give rise to and shape labour migration, and by control not the imposition of new discriminatory measures but greater effectiveness in administration. The following distinct but overlapping problems have to be tackled.

Illegal migration

Wherever there is still illegal migration it must be brought under control immediately. Otherwise all subsequent measures will be undermined (it is mainly illegal migration that gives rise to the worst forms of exploitation by intermediaries and employers). The onus here is largely on the receiving countries - and on all receiving countries acting together if this is to be tackled effectively - but it requires more than the abstract consent of sending countries. It requires the allocation of more money and more manpower and expertise to the control services.

It is sometimes feared that tighter control of emigration and/or immigration may increase the number of illegal immigrants. This is questionable, however, and evidence is scanty. It may well be that the detection rate would increase after tightening up without any increase in the actual number of illegal migrants. At any rate, the tangible and intangible over-all effects that might reasonably be expected from a tighter migration control may well outweigh the continued illegal migration of a tiny number of people.

International trafficking in labour and illegal migration are likely to form a major part of ILO's future concern in the field of migrant workers.[1]

Socially undesirable jobs

Immigration countries should look at the prime cause of contemporary labour migrations - the flight of indigenous workers from socially undesirable jobs.

The engagement of workers - both nationals and foreigners - for socially undesirable jobs must be more closely controlled and the jobs themselves must be made more desirable through social and financial revaluation.

As far as foreign workers are concerned, this means that wherever they are subject to labour market controls, applications for employment in socially undesirable jobs should be screened and not permitted as a matter of course. Where foreigners enjoy freedom of movement, other measures may be necessary to make it more expensive for employers to engage them for such jobs, for instance fiscal measures. The British Government has already made it clear that no more work permits will be issued for unskilled or semi-skilled industrial employment.[2] And the Minister of Finance of the Federal Republic of Germany stated in a recent

----

[1] Cf. ILO: Migrant workers, op. cit.

[2] See Department of employment gazette, February 1973, pp. 146-147.

interview that "in the Cabinet we are tending toward the view that employers must either supply sufficiently high living conditions for foreign workers, or they must learn to live without foreign workers".[1] The memorandum by the Bavarian Minister of the Interior already quoted[2] also implies a revision of policy along these lines.

A closer screening of applications for permits is suggested, perhaps initially for workplaces shunned by school-leavers. On a longer term basis, this requires thorough study of all the economic, technological, fiscal and social factors involved. The goal of such studies should be the progressive elimination of the category of "socially undesirable jobs" and the provision of better employment.

This necessitates a multilateral approach - because differential principles and timing may lead to trade distortion - along tripartite lines because the interests of employers and workers are closely affected.

Balancing skills and improving training of newly engaged foreign workers

The reduction of socially undesirable jobs is bound to be a slow and long-term process. As a complementary measure in the meantime, it is suggested that, wherever there is a labour shortage causing the employment of foreigners, a more controlled engagement policy should be pursued in terms of balancing skills and social status. For example, where a new factory is set up involving monotonous assembly-type work and where the white-collar and skilled jobs would be filled by nationals and the unskilled assembly jobs by foreigners, such a division of labour should be avoided as not being conducive to the public good - because it is conducive only to the formation of subproletariats, ghettos and prejudices. The principle of a more balanced engagement policy should cover all socially undesirable jobs, not only assembly work. It would mean that future engagements of foreigners should (through positive or negative incentives) take place only where a certain balance of higher status and lower status jobs for immigrants is kept.

This is not primarily a matter of making bilateral recruitment agreements or the EC's vacancy clearance system work more efficiently. More co-operation, better information, better selection and more appropriate placement are certainly basic requirements of a more controlled and balanced migration system. But they in themselves can be no

----

[1] The Times Business News, 26 January 1973; see also Süddeutsche Zeitung, 15 March 1973.

[2] See p. 90.

substitute for the political decision which is at the heart
of the matter and, if the problem is not tackled resolutely,
it will merely grow worse. There are two aspects to this
matter: (a) the deliberate decision to pursue a balanced
engagement policy; and (b) the decision to train migrants,
where necessary, to enable them to take up more highly
skilled positions.

In other words immigration countries must not only
engage, say, Spanish skilled workers, but must employ them
in appropriate positions. Where potential migrants have to
be trained prior to emigration (or prior to their
employment) receiving countries must be prepared to support
training courses (or induce employers to set up training
courses) on a much larger scale than hitherto, be it in the
country of origin or in the country of employment. This is
not a task which receiving countries should shoulder alone;
emigration countries should bear part of the costs, though
perhaps in the form of providing facilities rather than
money. The European Communities might consider this
training eligible for support from the European Social Fund.

In summary, it is suggested that a large-scale effort
be initiated to train potential migrant workers with a view
to breaking their typical engagement in low-status jobs and
to forestalling the consequent social problems, while at the
same time satisfying the continuing needs for more highly
skilled workers in receiving countries.

Social capital and social justice

Now that all major receiving countries have de facto
become countries of immigration - even though many are still
reluctant to face the fact - they ought to start treating
their immigrants as such and not as transients. The
receiving countries must not only be prepared to put up with
diminished returns from the employment of foreigners, they
must also be prepared to have these returns diminished even
further through investment in "unproductive" social capital
for immigrants.

That is to say, receiving countries must look after
the minorities which they have allowed in to work for them
and enable them to occupy a place in their societies which
is commensurate with their contributions and needs.
Otherwise they are conniving at creating the subproletariat
of tomorrow in the midst of their own societies, with
explosive implications in terms of class and ethnic strife.
As was said recently by the Director of Immigration in
France, many citizens in the receiving countries are
beginning to feel that it is "morally wrong to build the

development of our wealth on the backs of foreign manpower".[1]

Briefly, not one but two steps in the right direction are necessary. It is not enough formally to accord equal rights to non-nationals; these rights must be made socially meaningful. Specifically, the improvement of the material situation of migrants in need can be achieved only through positive discrimination - limited in time and purpose - to enable them to benefit from rights which are properly theirs.[2] These include the right of migrant families to live in decent surroundings and to advance educationally and occupationally.

Member countries of the European Communities might like to consider whether this could be financed from the European Social Fund, since supra-national measures designed for migrant workers regardless of nationality would not attract the same degree of opposition as national policies. Community-wide housing, language or training measures would not be discriminatory on grounds of nationality in the sense of entitling foreigners to something to which a national is not, for every national in need would be entitled to the same treatment as any foreigner in need. The European Communities have already had a forerunner of such a scheme in their housing programme for coal and steel workers in the ECSC. It should not be impossible to extend its principles to migrant workers in all occupations.

The fact that Sweden, Switzerland and Austria would not be covered by EC measures should not present any insurmountable obstacles. No country could afford to fall behind such standards for long, and these countries and their respective sending countries could follow the

----

[1] Quoted in The Times (J. Power, "Faulty Foundations for Europe's Growth"), 5 February 1973. The Times article echoed this in saying: "But clearly it cannot be good for us to feel that we can only develop our economy if we have a helot class available - a group of people who are identifiably of another race to do the despised menial jobs."

[2] As was stated recently in Le Monde (G. Mauco, "Les Travailleurs Etrangers"), 25-26 March 1973: "One cannot repeat too often that the foreign population needs an infra-structure in the realm of schooling, health, administration and housing that is better than that of the French population." And in the Federal Republic of Germany a memorandum of one of the main welfare organisations to the Government stated that the "rise to equality can only be achieved by putting migrants in a privileged position for a limited time". Arbeiterwohlfahrt Bundesverband: Denkschrift zur Reform der Ausländerpolitik (Bonn, 30 March 1973), p. 22.

principles of the Social Fund for purposes of tackling the social problems arising from immigration.

Return migration

The return of migrants who are skilled workers or who have benefited from the training measures suggested above would be a great asset to sending countries which are still developing. In principle, more pre-migration or pre-employment training might be expected to increase the numbers of those tending to settle in the receiving country. In empirical terms, however, it will increase the numbers of non-returnants only marginally, because those selected on account of their background for extensive training are likely to be potential settlers anyway. Nevertheless, there will be a significant proportion of returnants even among this group.

Early and more intensive study of the reasons for the failure of previous attempts to encourage the return of skilled workers is needed. There have been a number of co-operative schemes organised for returning Turkish workers and a Federal German/Turkish plan for highly skilled individuals which proved rather disappointing. What are the lessons to be learnt from these experiments? It might also be considered whether pre-migration training and return migration cannot be linked through financial sanctions such as repayment of training costs in cases of non-return, etc.[1]

Bringing the work to the worker

The preceding analysis has pointed out that labour migration is economically a tangible benefit to the receiving countries but socially rather a liability while, on the other hand, it does virtually nothing to help the development of the sending countries. In fact in some ways the situation comes near to being development aid in reverse. The analysis has also indicated the absurdity of a situation where masses of workers are transferred from countries lacking employment into generally labour-intensive industries which more often than not are protected by import duties, quotas or subsidies. Already there are plans in some receiving countries to recruit foreign manpower for relatively backward areas to which firms have been drawn by financial inducements designed to decentralise economic growth. One cannot evade the conclusion here that the transfer of jobs to the countries the migrants come from

----

[1] A "loyalty bonus" has been suggested by N. Falchi: "Per una 'politica dell'emigrazione'", _Studi Emigrazione_, Vol. 9, No. 25-26 (1972), pp. 92-111. This article carries some other detailed suggestions on training and return migration.

would be in many cases a more desirable solution for all
concerned.

Nowhere can a receiving country more easily put its
commitment to the promotion of employment opportunities in
developing countries into effect than by reviewing its subsidies or protection for transferable industries with large
foreign work forces where those countries can be equally
proficient - textiles and clothing being examples. Nowhere
can a receiving country more easily put its commitment to
higher living standards for its workers into effect than by
ending "subsidising an industry (textiles) whose products
often cost them (the workers) two, three, four times more
than imports from the Third World", as The Times recently
commented in relation to the end of 1972 meeting of the GATT
working party on textiles.[1]

A bare statement of this principle of course raises
more questions than it answers. Should the process of the
transfer of industries take place by lifting trade barriers
to the import of labour-intensive manufactures and semi-
manufactures and letting less viable undertakings die a
natural death? Should companies take the initiative in
opening subsidiary establishments in the less developed
countries and lay themselves open to the various types of
criticism levelled at multinational enterprises? Can
governments of industrialised countries be expected to
regard it as their function to give financial aid and
technical co-operation to strictly national enterprises in
the less-developed countries? And, within the context of
this chapter, is there any justification for giving priority
to the transfer of industries, where appropriate, to the
countries from which labour is at present imported rather
than to other countries?

In principle, the obligation of the industrialised
countries to facilitate exports from developing countries is
a general one, with the sole exception that specially
favourable treatment should go to the least developed
countries (none of which at present supply workers in any
quantities to Western Europe). Nor would it be appropriate
within the forum of the International Labour Organisation,
with its world vocation and its concern for employment
promotion in the parts of the world with the most serious
employment problems, to suggest priority for a particular
group of countries some of which do not rank very low in the
world development table. Yet some Western European
countries might wish to make a case for giving priority, at
least in the short term, to assisting the industrialisation
of those countries which supply them with labour as a means
of dealing with the problems described in this chapter.

----

[1] The Times (London), 10 January 1973.

EASTERN EUROPE

International migration of workers also takes place among the Socialist countries of Eastern Europe, though hitherto this has been on a smaller scale, has been in response to different forces and has taken somewhat different forms from those in Western Europe.

There is some movement of frontier workers which seems to derive from historical local situations and which is not markedly different from similar movements in Western Europe. For example, more than 5,000 male and 2,500 female Polish workers have traditionally been employed in the Czech border region. Hungary and Czechoslovakia entered into new arrangements about two years ago which provide for local contacts between district labour offices and a small amount of daily commuting in both directions. The German Democratic Republic had already asked for 1,500 Polish women to be employed in its border region in 1967.

Movements over longer distances are treated as a form of co-operation in the field of manpower utilisation within the framework of the general economic integration programme of the Council for Mutual Economic Assistance, improved international division of labour and specialisation among its member countries. In principle, they are regarded as short-term movements and not as permanent migration. In most cases, they take the form either of the export of specialised technical services (for instance in the field of construction) or of transfers of groups of workers which are primarily motivated by the objective of acquiring advanced training.[1]

As an example of the first form, Polish engineers and workers have participated in the construction of a steel works and an electricity generating station in the German Democratic Republic and of sugar refineries, a dam and glassworks in Czechoslovakia.

Some 12,000 Bulgarian construction and forestry workers are employed in undertakings in the USSR. Under economic integration plans, Bulgaria is to receive increased supplies of timber, paper, cellulose and cast-iron products from the USSR and it has accordingly furnished workers to construct the factories concerned. For some years, Bulgarian workers have been felling timber in the autonomous republic of Komi for export to Bulgaria.

----

[1] A general analysis of this subject is contained in an article "Enrichment on the basis of reciprocity" (in Russian) by T. Vais, research worker at the International Institute for Study of the Economic Problems of the World Socialist System, published in Sotsialisticheskaia industria (Moscow), 10 January 1973.

It is envisaged that exchanges of manpower of these kinds will in future play a more important part in the economic integration programme of the Council for Mutual Economic Assistance.

The German Democratic Republic is developing into a Socialist labour-importing country. Though official statistics are not available, the First Secretary of the Central Committee of the Socialist Unity Party of Germany, recently put the figure at 12,000 Polish and 13,000 Hungarian workers.[1] To these must be added an unknown number of Polish frontier workers. There are also a few thousand Russian specialists working in the German Democratic Republic, plus about 2,000 Czechoslovaks and 3,000 workers from the other East European countries, mainly Romanians.

The German Democratic Republic-Hungary manpower agreement dates back to 1967. It originally envisaged the employment of 2,500 young Hungarian workers for a period of two years in the electrical engineering, machine-building and other engineering industries, for the improvement of the workers' skills. In the meantime, 3,000-4,000 workers have been sent annually, between 25 per cent and 30 per cent of them women. It is also interesting to note that the original two-year contracts have been extended to three years. The number of Hungarian workers is due to be increased from the present 13,000 to 20,000 by 1975, and it is anticipated that the agreement will be extended to 1980 and put on a more reciprocal basis.

A recent meeting of the GDR-Hungarian Economic Committee noted that "this form of co-operation has proved a success. A great number of young Hungarian employees have been able to improve their skills, while at the same time this employment has contributed to the better use of existing productive capacity in economically important sectors of the GDR".[2]

The German Democratic Republic-Hungary arrangements provides that workers must receive the same wages and benefits as the local population plus extra time off and financial support when they go home on holiday. Forecast requirements are prepared 18 months in advance and vacancies are publicised in Hungary by the Ministry of Labour, whereupon it is up to the individual to apply. Preliminary language courses are organised in Hungary. Workers then travel and are accommodated in groups. The host country's employment authorities see to it that the factories carry out their obligations; and, on the Hungarian side, there is

----

[1] Interview with C.L. Sulzberger, in <u>Neues Deutschland</u>, 25 November 1972.

[2] Kommuniqué der XII. Tagung des Wirtschaftsaus-schusses DDR-UVR, in <u>Neues Deutschland</u>, 8 May 1973.

an embassy official who looks after individual welfare problems and complaints. After their return many Hungarian workers have found better jobs than they had before departure.

It is also noteworthy that agreements have been signed between Egypt on the one hand and Czechoslovakia and Bulgaria on the other for the employment of 15,000 and 10,000 Egyptian workers respectively in construction work. The Egyptians are to be employed under three-year contracts with free transport, equal wages and working conditions, and payment of part of their wages in convertible currency. The latter problem has so far prevented an agreement for the employment of Yugoslav workers in Czechoslovakia.

Projections of future labour market imbalances within Eastern Europe suggest that pressures exist which might lead to migrations increasing. L. Danieli[1] estimated that by 1980 the German Democratic Republic, Czechoslovakia and Hungary would at best just be able to manage with their labour force and, at worst, face a labour deficit in the region of 300,000-500,000 workers each. Bulgaria might be faced with either a smaller deficit or a small surplus. Poland and Romania, on her calculations, would be likely to experience labour surpluses in the region of 2.5 to 4 million workers. These projections might well be questioned by some of the governments concerned and, as a general principle, the Socialist governments reckon by judicious planning to arrive at a manpower balance within their own frontiers without having recourse to much immigration or emigration. However, the striking differences between countries suggest that there may be pressures for extended manpower co-operation among them, involving more exchange of workers than at present.

MIGRATION BETWEEN EASTERN AND
WESTERN EUROPE

As has been seen there is little movement of workers among Eastern European countries. There is even less between Eastern and Western Europe. This contrasts with the situation prior to 1939 when there was for instance at various periods considerable movement of Polish workers to Belgium, France and Germany (many of whom returned to their home country after 1945).[2]

The movements which take place today result not from bilateral agreements between governments but from contracts between undertakings in the two countries concerned. Thus

----

[1] L. Danieli, op. 164 cit., table 9, p. 164 et passim.

[2] The Polish Government has made it abundantly clear that it does not wish to return to this situation.

a limited number of engineers and technicians from Western European countries work temporarily in Eastern European countries on the installation or maintenance of equipment supplied by the companies employing them; their employment contracts remain with these companies and they do not become part of the labour force of the country in which they are working.

Similarly Eastern European undertakings carrying out contracts in Western Europe take their engineers and technicians with them. But there is an interesting additional development in regard to Polish and Romanian construction undertakings carrying out contracts in the Federal Republic of Germany in that they also take some of their skilled and unskilled workers with them (these undertakings sometimes operate as subcontractors but sometimes run the site on their own responsibility). The workers are paid the ruling local rate, partly in local currency, partly in their home currency (for the support of their dependants) and come and go with the undertaking which employs them. Little is published on this subject. The numbers involved are small - ranging from 1,000 to 2,000 each for Polish and Romanian workers. It is understood that some problems have arisen as regards the Polish workers, but that the Romanian undertakings and their workers feel generally that the exercise is successful.

This, as has been emphasised on all sides, involves very few workers. But it is a type of arrangement which avoids some of the pitfalls observed earlier in this chapter and there appears to be no a priori reason why the possibility of developing it further should not be explored.

There is also a small but interesting informal agreement between Romanian hotel undertakings and the Federal German authorities, under which Romanian hotel workers, mostly from the Black Sea region, work for roughly six months in the winter season in modern hotels in the Federal Republic in order to complete their training in hotel work and improve their knowledge of German. The workers are paid according to the local collective agreement. Between 200 and 300 workers a season are involved. Both sides are reported to be generally satisfied with the arrangement.

There are various joint ventures operated by the USSR and Finland on the two sides of their common frontier (such as the construction of atomic energy stations and of paper and cellulose factories and the laying of pipelines for natural gas) in which Soviet and Finnish workers work side by side. Further ventures of this kind are being negotiated.[1]

----

[1] Report in Pravda, 5 April 1973, of a speech made by President Podgorny in Helsinki.

In none of these cases is the number of workers involved large, but the arrangements all demonstrate that successful manpower co-operation between countries of Eastern and Western Europe is possible.

In addition, within the framework of industrial co-operation, there are instances of Western manufacturers subcontracting the production of certain parts or the carrying-out of certain processes to undertakings in Eastern countries; some of these arrangements might yield interesting lessons on ways of "taking the work to the worker" as an alternative to migration, to which reference was made earlier in this chapter.

With the advent of closer contacts between East and West, the number and importance of these types of arrangement are likely to grow and new possibilities may be opened up. As an example of these, mention may be made of the suggestion presented at the 58th Session of the International Labour Conference, June 1973, by the Polish Minister of Labour, Wages and Social Affairs that future forms of European co-operation should include the possibility of the exchange of young workers.

CHAPTER V

SUGGESTED THEMES FOR DISCUSSION

After taking a rapid look at the main changes in the employment field in Europe, this report has examined three groups of problems which, though at first sight distinct, have many links.

If there is one *leitmotiv* it is that the new generations entering the labour market, with their higher average level of education, aspire to easier, more pleasant and better-paid jobs, leaving the dirty jobs to others. In a number of West European countries, this has been possible only because of the continuous influx of foreign workers. These countries are beginning to see the disadvantages of letting the influx continue at its present rate, yet at the same time they are proposing to devote ever-increasing resources to educational expansion which, if it means acceleration of the present tendency, can only aggravate the problem. Educational expansion cannot be put into reverse, but its course can be changed so that it contributes more to, and conflicts less with, employment policy aims. Greater flexibility in patterns of working life, offering more possibilities of alternating work and study, opens up one path of action; it also has far-reaching implications over the whole employment field, in fact over virtually all the fields of labour, social security and income distribution with which the ILO is concerned and it may well become one of the major issues facing many European countries in the near future.

The centrally-planned economies face similar problems of meeting both the rising educational aspirations of their peoples and the demand for rapidly improving consumption standards with a labour force which in some cases is growing scarcely at all. Revision of the educational system is in the air, and is directed towards ways of combining satisfaction of these aspirations with a more effective contribution to the achievement of employment aims.

Implications of changes in the last decade

The last decade has seen far-reaching changes in the employment scene in Europe such as:

(a)   a decline of employment in the primary sector, diminished relative importance of employment in the secondary sector, and expansion of employment in the tertiary sector;

(b)   within each sector, a rapid change in structure and
        technology (sometimes inseparable one from the other)
        which has radically affected the numbers and types of
        workers needed and led to an increasing element of
        mismatch;

(c)   a change in the character of the labour force
        resulting from demographic trends, longer education
        (with a consequent rise in educational levels and job
        aspirations), higher participation rates of women with
        family responsibilities (with a consequent increase in
        demand for part-time or intermittent jobs and more
        flexible schedules) and more students and pensioners
        being interested in temporary or part-time employment;
        and

(d)   internationalisation of many of the problems as a
        result of expansion of trade and easier communi-
        cations; in several Western European countries, a
        growing dependence for labour in certain sectors on
        migrant workers, including some from outside Europe;
        and in some of the countries supplying these workers,
        a growing dependence on outlets in Western Europe for
        their surplus manpower.

These changes are not of recent origin, and their general
lines are well known. In fact, there is a danger that
repeated generalised reference to them may blunt interest in
the subject. This would be undesirable, as many of the
changes are not being monitored or analysed closely enough,
and are not being sufficiently explained to the public; nor
are their long-term implications for policy, not only as
regards employment, but in other fields such as education,
being sufficiently taken into account. Old assumptions
still colour some thinking on employment matters.

        For instance, the muscular male workers of the Albert
Thomas memorial are no longer truly representative of
Europe's workers. Some such workers of course still exist
(though in several countries, there is a strong likelihood
that they will be foreigners). Typical European workers
today would include, to take a very few examples, an
electronic technician maintaining complex medical
instrumentation in a public hospital, a mother of young
schoolchildren working only at peak hours at the check-out
desk of a supermarket, and a student doing vacation work as
receptionist on a camping site. Yet there is still
sometimes a tendency to think of the regular full-time
manual worker in industry as the person with whom employment
administrators should really be concerned (for instance,
when additional employment is required in a development
area, there is a tendency to think almost exclusively of
attracting new manufacturing industry to the area). In the
future, manufacturing industry in Europe is likely to offer
fewer and fewer jobs, as it becomes technologically more
advanced and structurally more concentrated, and as

competing industries in East Asia and in certain countries of Latin America take over. Employment policy should be concerned with the total labour needs of the economy, with employment opportunities for the whole labour force and with attempting to bring about the closest possible match between the two.

Employment authorities have a better understanding of this objective than, say, ten years ago, but it cannot be said that in general they have developed adequate measures to improve the match between jobs and workers, or to intervene rapidly to make necessary adjustments on the labour market. Even in Sweden, which has been several years ahead of other countries in Western Europe in analysing its labour market problems, in devising programmes to deal with them, and in providing resources to carry them out, problems of mismatch have continued to arise. To take another illustration, the National Economic Development Office in the United Kingdom foresaw a year ago that a revival of economic activity would already start to run into a shortage of skilled workers while the number of registered unemployed was still over half a million, and this is now happening. One remedy suggested for this sort of situation (which is not limited to one country) is to concentrate training and retraining during periods of recession so that skilled workers will be available when recovery comes, but not much effort has yet been applied to putting this into practice.

Without more effective action, it seems possible that the future employment situation in some European countries will show the following characteristics:

(a)   more residual unemployment, perhaps of longer duration, especially for older workers, and especially in areas of declining industry;

(b)   more bottlenecks due to shortages of certain types of skilled workers or shortages of persons willing to take unpleasant or low-status jobs;

(c)   as a result of the pressing need to meet the latter type of shortage, the haphazard sucking-in of more migrant workers, possibly from countries further and further afield, with resulting economic and social problems for both receiving and sending countries;

(d)   among young people, an increasing proportion of each age cohort continuing full-time education up to the age of 22 or even 25 and finishing up more and more in jobs which do not make use of what they have learnt and which they find frustrating.

Is this picture too sombre?

More flexible patterns of working life

It has been suggested in Chapter II that one approach to some of these problems might be made through encouraging more flexible patterns of working life; for instance, by providing recurrent education and training when and where it is needed, so that the individual can better meet the current needs of the labour market, and by making more imaginative arrangements for helping such people as women with family responsibilities or workers of pensionable age to obtain the sort of employment they would like.

Proposals for more flexibility in working life are not normally put forward on these grounds; rather they are seen as a way of improving the quality of working life by giving the individual greater control over the disposal of his or her working years. They also open up interesting prospects of a greater variety of ways in which leisure could be distributed over an individual's life. This is a topic which deserves extensive examination in the context of humanisation of work. However, for the purposes of this report, it is suggested that discussion might be centred on the contribution which greater flexibility of working life might make to the solution of current employment problems and on an attempt to answer some of the questions put at the beginning of Chapter II. Is there a rational basis for the current sequence of education, training, work and retirement? Are there any real obstacles to the loosening up of this sequence? In particular, what more can be done to help women who have temporarily withdrawn from the labour force in order to bring up a young family, prepare for a new career? What more can be done to permit freer mobility between occupations, employers and industries without falling into the trap of excessive labour turnover? Should any special measures be taken to make better use of the work potential of "marginal" youth? What more can be done to help older workers who wish either to retire before the normal pensionable age or to continue working after that age?

The expansion of higher education and employment

There has always been a certain amount of mismatch, quantitative and qualitative, between the skills demanded by the economy at any given moment and the skills actually available among workers; a new and serious problem of educational mismatch has been added in many European countries following the rapid expansion of higher education in response to the social aspirations of the population rather than to the needs of the labour market. The number of graduates in many disciplines is increasing faster than the demand in the occupations traditionally filled by them. As a result, they are more and more having to accept jobs below their salary and career expectations. Some aspects of this problem have been discussed in Chapter III. Higher education in excess of labour market needs may be fully justified on social and cultural grounds; but this needs to be fully recognised and its implications for employment and social policy reassessed.

In the Socialist countries, the intake into higher education is more closely related to foreseen needs, but even in a strictly planned economy, this method of control is not giving entire satisfaction in that technological changes sometimes leads to undertakings finding that they are no longer able to employ the number and types of graduates they had planned for, and in that some graduates consider their qualifications are not being properly utilised in the jobs to which they have been appointed. In market economies, where forecasting is inevitably less precise because the demand for graduates is affected by more external influences, a similarly strict control of intake in relation to forecast needs would be both more difficult to introduce and less likely to meet with success.

In these circumstances, it seems desirable to give much fuller consideration to the progressive replacement of the present form of lengthy, uninterrupted higher education following on secondary schooling by a system of recurrent education involving primarily the alternation of study with work, thus providing a better link between education and the economy and more educational opportunities for the individual. Because of its newness and complexity, this subject needs of course to be given much more thought and more experimentation.

Migration policy

Another trend which it is now generally recognised cannot be allowed to continue unchecked is the mass movement of migrant workers into low-status jobs in several West European countries. Some of the problems to which this has already given rise, in both the sending and the receiving countries, have been described in Chapter IV. Unless something is done soon, these problems will get worse. Yet, properly organised, migration will for a long time continue to have a useful part to play in meeting the employment difficulties of both types of country.

There is now widespread agreement that better control or better channelling of the movement of workers is needed if the negative aspects of migration are to be diminished while its positive aspects are to be retained. The question is: How is this to be done without depriving the economies of each type of country of the workers they need, and without depriving the individual of the right to leave his country if he thinks he can thereby improve his economic and social lot?

The ILO has already been asked to take action on trafficking in migrant workers and this is one of the matters which will be touched on in the discussion of the subject of migrant workers at the International Labour Conference in 1974. This is however only a small part of the problem (at least, in Europe). More important seems to

be the need for better control at source of the demand for
foreign workers which creates these flows. Can some of the
low-status jobs be either eliminated or upgraded by
technological development or better work organisation?
Would it be desirable for employers to be charged the real
social cost of a migrant worker - for instance is there a
case for a special payroll tax for migrant employees, the
proceeds being applied to covering the extra infrastructure
costs to which they give rise? Where the demand arises in
manufacturing industry, cannot the question be asked whether
it is still appropriate that the industry should be kept
alive in the country concerned? What are the possibilities
of transferring all or some manufacturing processes to
countries with labour surpluses (though not necessarily to
those from which the migrant workers come)? If employment
cannot be transferred (as for instance in the case of most
construction and service employment), what are the prospects
of raising the productivity, remuneration and status of
migrant workers so that the gap between them and the
national workers is narrowed? Can the seniority pattern
among migrant workers be improved by engaging more of them
for senior positions and by giving others special training
opportunities and better chances of promotion? Can their
effective voice in collective bargaining be improved? Many
of these questions go beyond the traditional boundaries of
employment policy, but they need to be answered if a
rational and consistent policy for the employment of
migrants is to be established.

As has been shown in Chapter IV, there is no clear
distinction between the temporary and the permanent migrant.
One may become the other. Nevertheless, migration policy
might be based on the idea that there are three diverse
streams which have different weights in different receiving
countries according to the structure of the economy, and the
nationality composition of the migrants. Firstly, there are
seasonal migration streams. Secondly, there are streams of
predominantly young and predominantly single people who
migrate with a fixed objective and intend, on attaining it,
to return home. Thirdly, there are a great number who have
neither a fixed aim nor a definite time horizon, who simply
want to get along as well as possible and preferably stay
united with their families. Migrants of the third type tend
to settle down as established members of the national labour
force of the receiving country. Sending and receiving
countries would probably both like to see the second stream
dominant, but in practice little is done to encourage this.

Would it not be possible to do more from the outset to
steer migrants into the second stream? For instance, by
selecting young single workers for preference, by
encouraging them to keep in touch with the needs of their
home country, by seeing that they get some training with a
view to returning home, by incentives to return, and by
administrative measures to tell them of employment
opportunities at home? These ideas are not new, and

experience with putting them into effect has not been very promising, but there seems to be a case for persisting with more experiments. The experience of the Socialist countries (though it presumes compulsory rather than voluntary rotation) should not be excluded from examination solely because of the difference in economic systems. The general loosening-up of the pattern of working life envisaged in Chapter II may make the process of voluntary rotation easier in the furture than it has been in the past.

Recommendations for future ILO activities in these fields

It is hoped that discussion of these themes will lead to the European members of the ILO indicating to what extent they would wish the ILO to undertake any future European-centred activities in any or all of these fields, and in what form.

Several of the topics are already the concern of various European regional organisations (or of organisations like OECD and CMEA which are predominantly European in membership) and Members would undoubtedly wish to avoid duplicating work already being done by these bodies.

The ILO can however perform a useful task in providing a forum for more constant and effective interchange of information and experience between these organisations, the continent's market economies and its centrally planned economies in regard to technical problems of the types discussed in this report which arise in both types of country. Such problems might concern for instance the many issues involved in giving greater flexibility to patterns of working life; these include the general question of the desirability and feasibility of the various forms of flexibility discussed in Chapter II as well as specific points such as ways of organising a better sequence of education and employment, better ways of helping women to re-enter employment which will give them greater equality of opportunity with men than they enjoy at present, and better ways of easing the transition of aging workers from their accustomed job to a situation in which they can choose the combination of work and leisure which suits each individual best.

The education-labour market relationship raises an immense number of issues, many of which have so far scarcely been touched. For instance, what are the factors determining graduates' expectations? How can the frustrations resulting from disappointed expectations be reduced? What are the alternative forms of post-secondary education which might better meet the needs of the employment market while still leaving a wide range of educational paths open to the individual? Is employer-sponsoring of students an effective way of relating studies to employment needs and is there scope for its extension? How can employers improve their planning for the recruitment and career advancement of graduates? Inter-occupational mobility and the scope for the substitution of graduates for non-graduates and vice versa could also be looked into.

Among the many problems concerning the place of migration in employment policy, there would seem to be a need above all in the coming years for the evaluation of successes and failures in taking work to the workers as an alternative to international migration, of arrangements to make return migration more attractive to the migrant and more beneficial to the sending country and, in the latter connection, of ways of putting migrants' remittances to better use.

Several of these problems are not exclusive to Europe, though European countries may be the most involved. Questions of flexible patterns of working life and of the education-labour market relationship affect industrialised countries in other parts of the world too. Questions of migrant workers in Europe affect also the countries of North Africa which send, or are contemplating sending, workers to Europe. The European constituents of the ILO might therefore consider that, while some questions should be examined on a strictly European basis, in others it would be desirable to associate other interested countries.

After dealing with the question of the priorities which might be given to the various subjects, there remains the question of the form which activities on these subjects might take. It will no doubt be difficult for the Conference to give very precise guidance on this point in the absence of precise indications of the resources likely to be available. The most reasonable assumption may be that some resources will be available, but on a scale which will require their most economical use.

The possible forms of activity might include (1) the preparation and subsequent publication of studies on specific European topics such as those raised earlier in this Chapter; (2) meetings of technical experts from representative European countries on very precisely defined aspects of these topics; and (3) the consideration of such topics and the reports of such meetings at further European tripartite meetings.

These suggestions are not exhaustive and many others may be made in the course of the Conference.

To which topics in the employment field should the ILO's future European activities be directed? What form should these activities take? What contribution to them are the European countries prepared to make?

These are not matters on which there would be any point in the Conference considering formal resolutions at

this stage. They call for detailed examination and not
merely general debate, but the outcome of the discussion
might well take the form of an agreed report indicating the
degree of consensus and the matters on which there are
differences of view. On the basis of such a report, it will
be possible to consider the scope for further action.

Table 1

Projected Annual Rates of Growth of Total
Labour Force by Major Areas 1960-1980
(percentages)

Major Area	1960-65	1965-70	1970-75	1975-80
Europe (excl. USSR)	0.66	0.51	0.62	0.54
USSR	1.04	1.19	1.48	1.27
Asia	1.84	1.87	1.92	1.91
Africa	1.90	2.07	2.18	2.30
Northern America	1.38	1.67	1.66	1.55
Latin America	2.28	2.37	2.55	2.58
Oceania	2.17	2.19	2.20	2.09
World	1.60	1.66	1.76	1.74

Source: ILO: Labour Force Projections 1965-1985, Part V,
Geneva 1971, table 4.

Table 2

Europe: Annual Rate of Growth of the Labour Force
(percentages)

Regions and Countries	1960-1970	1970-1980
Northern and Western Europe		
Austria	-0.2	0.4
Belgium	0.4	0.5
Denmark	0.8	0.6
Finland	1.0	0.6
France	1.1	0.7
Germany (Fed. Rep. of)	0.3	0.4
Ireland	0.1	0.8
Luxembourg	1.0	1.1
Netherlands	1.6	1.0
Norway	0.6	0.4
Sweden	0.9	0.4
Switzerland	1.4	0.8
United Kingdom	0.4	0.2
Eastern Europe		
Bulgaria	0.7	0.3
Czechoslovakia	0.7	0.4
Germany (Dem. Rep. of)	-0.8	0.5
Hungary	0.5	0.1
Poland	1.5	1.5
Romania	0.8	0.6
Southern Europe		
Greece	0.5	0.6
Italy	0.1	0.6
Malta	0.7	-0.1
Portugal	0.1	-0.2
Spain	0.5	0.6
Turkey	1.9	2.2
Yugoslavia	1.0	1.0
USSR	1.1	1.4

Source: ILO: Labour Force Projections 1965-1985, Part IV:
Europe, Northern America, Oceania and USSR,
Geneva 1971, tables 1 and 4. (For Turkey, see
Part I.)

Table 3

Europe: Gross[a] Activity Rates by Sex, 1960 to 1980

(percentages)

Regions and Countries	Total of Both Sexes			Males			Females		
	1960	1970	1980	1960	1970	1980	1960	1970	1980
Northern and Western Europe									
Austria	48.0	44.8	44.4	61.5	56.8	55.6	36.2	34.1	34.3
Belgium	38.7	38.1	38.3	58.5	55.2	53.6	19.7	21.6	23.6
Denmark	45.7	45.9	45.2	63.6	62.0	58.9	28.0	30.1	31.6
Finland	45.8	47.4	48.1	57.6	59.4	59.6	34.8	36.1	37.2
France	43.1	42.9	42.3	59.1	57.7	56.0	28.1	28.6	28.8
Germany (Fed. Rep. of)	47.7	44.8	44.6	64.0	59.4	57.8	33.2	31.4	32.1
Ireland	39.4	38.2	37.2	58.2	54.9	52.9	20.5	21.3	21.3
Luxembourg	41.4	40.9	41.2	61.5	59.3	58.1	21.8	22.6	23.4
Netherlands	36.6	37.8	37.6	57.1	57.4	56.9	16.2	18.5	18.5
Norway	39.2	38.4	36.3	60.7	58.4	54.7	17.9	18.5	18.0
Sweden	43.3	44.1	43.3	61.1	59.4	56.4	25.6	28.7	30.2
Switzerland	46.2	45.4	43.7	65.9	63.3	60.0	27.3	28.1	28.0
United Kingdom	46.3	47.1	43.3	65.0	61.6	57.9	28.8	29.3	29.2
Eastern Europe									
Bulgaria	53.9	53.3	51.2	62.2	61.4	58.9	45.7	47.3	43.3
Czechoslovakia	48.8	48.5	47.1	59.7	59.2	57.3	38.4	38.2	37.2
Germany (Dem. Rep. of)	49.8	45.8	46.8	62.4	57.7	58.1	39.5	35.7	36.6
Hungary	49.1	49.8	47.9	65.9	66.0	62.6	33.4	34.7	33.9
Poland	47.8	49.6	51.9	55.9	57.1	59.3	40.1	42.5	44.7
Romania	57.1	56.1	53.7	64.5	63.4	60.8	50.1	49.0	46.6
Southern Europe									
Greece	45.2	44.4	44.1	63.7	62.0	60.9	27.7	27.7	27.9
Italy	40.4	37.8	37.2	61.9	57.7	54.9	19.7	18.9	20.1
Malta	29.9	33.9	35.9	49.6	55.0	57.2	11.9	14.6	16.6
Portugal	37.4	34.8	31.9	63.6	59.4	54.1	13.2	12.4	11.9
Spain	38.1	36.5	35.2	64.3	61.4	58.8	13.4	13.1	12.9
Turkey	48.2	44.8	42.6	57.4	54.2	51.4	38.6	35.1	33.6
Yugoslavia	45.4	44.9	44.8	60.3	59.6	59.5	31.1	30.6	30.2
USSR	51.5	50.8	52.2	55.2	55.1	57.0	48.5	47.1	48.0

[a] Total labour force: total population.

Source: ILO, Labour Force Projections, 1965-1985, Part IV: Europe, Northern America, Oceania and USSR, Geneva 1971, tables 2 and 5. (For Turkey see Part I.)

Table 4

Europe: Participation in Economic Activity of Females,
20-49 Years Old, 1960 and 1970 or Nearest Date:
Selected Countries

(percentages)

Country	Year of Reference	Type of Data[a]	20-24 years	25-29 years	30-49 years
Bulgaria	1956	R	69.0	69.3	75.1
	1965	R	72.1	83.8	86.1
Czechoslovakia	1961[b,h]	R	69.2	57.9	64.7
	1970[b,h]	R	78.7	79.3	79.4
Denmark	1960	R	58.9	38.7	36.5
	1965	R	61.9	45.5	45.9
Finland	1960[b]	R	60.7	56.9	58.0
	1970[b]	R	62.6	67.7	66.7
France[c]	1962	R	61.8	45.6	41.1
	1968	R	62.3	50.7	43.2
Hungary[d]	1960[b]	R	55.3	48.7	50.2
	1970[b]	R	66.5	65.7	68.4
Italy[e]	1960	ESMO	48.3	36.2	33.6
	1970	ESMO	43.3	33.2	29.9
Luxembourg[d]	1960[f]	R	49.2	29.4	27.2
	1966	R	50.7	31.5	26.3
Romania	1956	R	78.1	74.3	74.5
	1966	R	74.3	78.5	77.9
Sweden[g]	1960	R	57.3	42.0	36.1
	1965	R	56.2	44.5	46.5
Switzerland	1960	R	69.9	43.2	30.6
	1970	R	71.4	51.1	44.5

[a] R: Census; ESMO: Labour force sample survey.

[b] Provisional results based on sample tabulation of censure returns.

[c] Figures based on 5 per cent sample tabulation of census returns in 1962 and on a 25 per cent sample tabulation in 1968.

[d] Not including persons seeking work for the first time.

[e] Annual average of quarterly surveys.

[f] Not including unemployed.

[g] Not including persons seeking work for the first time.

[h] Not including unpaid workers in agriculture.

Source: ILO, Year Book of Labour Statistics (1965-1972 editions) and national statistical year books.

Table 5

Europe: Employed Civilian Labour Force by Major Sector of Economic Activity
in 1960 and 1970 or Nearest Dates: Selected Countries

Regions and Countries	Date of Reference[a]	Type of Data[b]	Type of Industrial Classification[c]	Sectors of Activity			
				Total of Three Sectors	Percentages		
					Agriculture	Industries	Services[d]
Northern and Western Europe							
Austria	1960	EO	A	3 289	24.2	39.7	36.1
	1970[e]	ESMO	A	2 974	19.4	40.6	40.0
Belgium[f]	1960	EO	A	3 447	8.7	46.8	44.6
	1970	EO	A	3 747	4.8	44.7	50.4
Denmark	1960	R	A	1 984	18.5	37.4	44.2
	1970	ESMO	B	2 325	11.4	38.5	50.1
Finland	1960	ESMO	A	2 087	36.4	31.9	31.7
	1970	ESMO	A	2 142	22.7	35.5	41.8
France	1960	EO	A	18 712	22.4	37.8	39.8
	1970	EO	A	20 410	14.0	38.9	47.1
Germany (Fed. Rep. of)	1960	EO	A	25 954	14.0	48.8	37.3
	1970	EO	A	26 705	9.0	50.3	40.7
Ireland	1960	EO	A	1 046	37.3	23.7	39.0
	1970	EO	A	1 053	27.6	30.1	42.3
Luxembourg	1960	EO	A	133	16.4	44.1	39.6
	1970	EO	A	143	10.8	46.7	42.5
Netherlands[g]	1960	EO	A	4 052	11.5	42.3	46.2
	1970	EO	A	4 567	7.2	41.0	51.8
Norway	1960	EO	A	1 395	21.6	35.6	42.9
	1970	EO	A	1 497	13.9	37.3	48.8
Sweden[h]	1962	ESMO	A	3 621	13.1	42.0	45.0
	1970	ESMO	A	3 854	8.2	38.4	53.5
Switzerland[e]	1960	R	B	2 508	11.2	50.5	38.3
	1970	R	B	3 005	7.6	48.3	44.1
United Kingdom	1960	EO	A	24 257	4.2	48.8	41.1
	1970	EO	A	24 709	2.9	46.6	50.6
Eastern Europe							
Bulgaria	1956	R	C	4 150	64.2	18.6	17.2
	1965	R	C	4 268	44.3	33.4	22.3
Czechoslovakia[k]	1960	EO	B	6 028	26.1	45.9	21.1
	1970	EO	B	6 984	18.4	46.5	35.0
Germany (Dem. Rep.)[j]	1960	EO	C	7 686	17.0	47.5	35.5
	1970	EO	C	7 769	12.8	49.1	38.1
Hungary[e]	1960	R	A	4 710	39.8	36.2	24.0
	1970[i]	R	A	4 984	24.7	45.3	30.1
Romania	1956	R	C	10 378	70.1	16.8	13.1
	1966	R	C	10 356	57.2	25.2	17.7
Southern Europe							
Greece[e]	1961[i]	EO	B	3 517	55.7	19.8	25.4
	1971	EO	B	3 222	41.3	26.1	32.6
Italy	1960	ESMO	A	20 002	32.8	36.9	30.2
	1970	ESMO	A	18 774	19.6	43.7	36.7
Malta[e]	1957	R	B	91	10.6	38.1	51.3
	1967	R	B	94	8.1	39.3	52.7
Portugal[l]	1960	R	A	3 126	42.8	29.5	27.7
	1970	EO	A	3 030	33.0	35.7	31.2
Spain	1960	EO	A	11 474	42.3	32.0	25.7
	1970	EO	A	12 372	29.6	37.4	33.0
Yugoslavia[e]	1961[i,m]	R	C	7 960	59.7	23.0	17.3
	1971	R	C	8 114	48.4	29.7	21.9

[a] ma = annual average or mid-year estimate.
[b] EO = official estimates; ESMO = labour force sample survey; and R : census.
[c] A : International Standard Industrial Classification of All Economic Activities, 1968 edition (new ISIC);
B : ISIC, 1958 edition; and C : national classification of economic activities. Sectoral data obtained from branches of economic activity of these three classifications are not strictly comparable. Between A and B, however, the differences are unimportant and are found in the sectors of "Industry" and "Services". Between C and A and B, differences can sometimes be important and concern the three sectors.
[d] The "Services" sector and consequently the "total" of the three sectors sometimes include "activities not adequately described".
[e] Including armed forces.
[f] Including apprentices.
[g] Man-Years.
[h] Employed civilian labour force 16 to 74 years old.
[i] Provisional figures based on a sample tabulation of census returns.
[j] Not including apprentices.
[k] Not including family workers and apprentices.
[l] Including career soldiers.
[m] Not including nationals working abroad.

Sources : ILO, Year Book of Labour Statistics (editions from 1965 to 1972); OECD, Labour Force Statistics, 1959-1970, Paris, 1972; and national statistical year books.

Table 6.a

Northern, Western and Southern Europe - Civilian Labour Force by Status
1960 and 1970 or Nearest Dates: Selected Countries

Regions and Countries	Date of Reference[a]	Type of Data[b]	Total[c]	Status		
				Percentages		
				Wage and Salary earners	Employers and workers on own account	Family Workers
Northern and Western Europe						
Austria[d]	1961	R	3 370	70.8	15 8	13.4
	1971	ESMO	2 986	74.1	} 25.9	
Belgium[e]	1960	EO	3 447	73.8	19.5	6.7
	1970	EO	3 747	79.3	15.9	4.8
Denmark	1960	R	2 080	77.6	} 22.4	
	1970	ESMO	2 325	79.7	15.0	5.3
Finland	1960	R	2 026	65.6	19.5	14.9
	1970	ESMO	2 142	76.3	12.1	11.6
France	1960	EO	18 712	69.5	30.5	
	1970	EO	20 410	77.8	22.2	
Germany (Fed. Rep. of)	1960	EO	25 954	77.2	12.7	10.1
	1970	EO	26 705	82.1	10.9	7.0
Ireland	1961	R	1 044	61.4	27.4	11.2
	1970	EO	1 058	69.0	} 31.0	
Luxembourg	1960	EO	134	70.5	16.7	12.8
	1960	EO	144	76.4	13.2	10.4
Netherlands[f]	1960	EO	4 052	78.1	21.9	
	1970	EO	4 567	83.3	16.7	
Norway	1960	EO	1 395	74.3	21.8	3.9
	1970	EO	1 497	80.4	17.9	1.7
Sweden	1960[h]	R	3 226	83.2	14.0	2.8
	1970[i]	ESMO	3 854	89.1	8.8	2.1
United Kingdom	1960	EO	24 257	92.7	7.3	g
	1970	EO	24 709	92.6	7.4	g
Southern Europe						
Greece[j]	1961	R	3 537	34.5	36.1	29.4
	1971[k]	R	3 244	40.0	} 60.0	
Italy	1960	ESMO	20 002	58.4	25.9	15.7
	1970	ESMO	18 774	68.3	23.6	8.1
Malta[d]	1957	R	91	70.9	24.8	4.3
	1967	R	94	75.0	22.0	3.0
Portugal[j]	1960	R	3 126	74.3	25.7	
	1970	EO	3 030	75.9	24.1	
Spain	1960	EO	11 474	61.0	39.0	
	1970	EO	12 372	64.4	35.6	

a ma : Annual average or mid-year estimate.
b EO : Official estimate; ESMO : Labour force sample survey and R : census.
c Not including the category "Others or status unknown".
d Including armed forces.
e Including apprentices.
f Man-Year.
g Figures not available.
h Including persons unemployed for less than four months.
i Employed civilian labour force from 16 to 74 years old.
j Including career soldiers.
k Provisional figures based on sample tabulation of census returns.

Sources : ILO, Year Boook of Labour Statistics (1965-1972 editions); OECD, Labour Force Statistics, 1959-1970, Paris, 1972

Table 6.b

Eastern Europe: Labour Force by Status 1960 and 1970
or Nearest Dates

Selected Countries

Country	Year of Reference	Type of Data[a]	Total[b]	Status		
					Percentage	
				Wage and salary earners	Members of Producers' Co-operatives	Employers and workers on own account and family workers
Bulgaria	1956	R	4 150	36.7	42.7	20.6
	1965	R	4 265	57.3	41.4	1.3
Germany, Democratic Republic[c]	1960	EO	7 686	80.7	13.8	5.5
	1970	EO	7 769	83.6	13.0	3.4
Hungary	1960	R	4 876	63.7	13.4	22.9
	1970[d]	R	5 001	78.0	18.8	3.2
Romania	1956	R	10 447	30.5	8.5	61.0
	1966	R	10 360	44.5	47.9	7.6

[a] $\underline{EO}$: official estimate; and $\underline{R}$: census.

[b] Not including "status unknown".

[c] Not including apprentices.

[d] Provisional figures based on sample tabulation of census returns.

Sources: ILO: Year Book of Labour Statistics (1965-1972 editions) and national statistical year books.

Table 7

Europe: Unemployment Trends, 1960-1971, Selected Countries

(thousands)

Regions and Countries	Source of Data[a]	1960	1961	1962	1963	1964	1965	1966	1967	1968	1969	1970	1971
Northern and Western Europe													
Austria	IVB	82.3	63.5	64.7	70.6	65.8	65.5	61.4	64.6	70.8	67.1	58.4	52.0
Belgium[b]	IVB	162.3	129.4	109.4	109.3	77.1	92.2	97.2	131.2	142.7	120.6	102.8	107.9
Denmark[c]	III	31.0	24.0	22.0	32.0	18.5	16.1	18.3	21.8	38.7	31.2	23.9	30.0
Finland	I	31.0	27.0	27.0	32.0	33.0	31.0	35.0	63.0	89.0	62.0	41.0	49.0
France	IVB	130.1	111.1	122.6	140.3	114.1	142.1	147.7	196.0	253.8	223.0	262.1	338.2
Germany (Fed. Rep. of)	IVB	237.4	161.1	142.4	174.2	157.4	139.2	154.3	444.6	313.6	173.2	143.8	177.8
Ireland[d,e]	IVA	52.9	46.6	46.6	50.0	48.9	49.4	47.7	55.0	58.3	57.3	64.9	62.0
Luxembourg	IVB	0.1	0.1	0.1	0.2	0.1	0.1	-	0.2	0.1	-	-	-
Netherlands[f]	IVB	30.1	22.4	22.7	25.0	22.1	26.7	37.3	78.5	71.9	52.9	46.4	62.0
Norway	IVB	17.1	13.0	15.2	17.7	15.5	13.4	11.9	11.4	16.5	15.6	12.5	12.2
Sweden[h]	I	.	.	56.0	65.0	58.0	44.0	59.0	79.0	85.0	73.0	59.0	101.0
Switzerland	IVB	1.2	0.7	0.6	0.8	0.3	0.3	0.3	0.3	0.3	0.2	0.1	0.1
United Kingdom[g]	IVB	377.2	346.5	467.4	558.0	404.4	347.1	361.0	558.8	586.0	580.9	618.0	799.1
Southern Europe													
Greece	IVB	92.6	79.9	79.2	75.6	70.8	69.5	69.7	89.5	78.1	70.7	52.1	
Italy	I	836.0	710.0	611.0	504.0	549.0	721.0	769.0	689.0	694.0	663.0	615.0	613.0
Malta	IVB	3.4	4.0	5.6	6.8	7.1	8.2	7.8	5.7	4.8	3.8	3.9	5.3
Spain	IVB	114.4	124.6	97.8	100.2	129.6	147.1	123.2	146.3	182.0	158.9	145.6	190.3
Yugoslavia	IVB	159.2	191.3	236.6	230.3	212.5	237.0	257.6	269.1	311.0	330.6	319.6	291.3

Symbols: . Figures not available.

- Magnitude nil (or negligible).

[a] I - Labour force sample surveys.

III - Trade union and trade union benefit funds statistics.

IVA - Employment office statistics (applicants for work).

IVB - Employment office statistics (unemployed persons registered).

[b] Wholly unemployed in receipt of benefit as well as average daily number of partially unemployed.

[c] Unemployment among members of trade union benefit funds.

[d] Registered applicants for work remaining unplaced.

[e] Series revised since 1966.

[f] Since 1968, including married women who are not heads of households.

[g] Wholly unemployed.

[h] Persons from 16-74 years old. (1962 and 1963: 14 years and over.)

Source: Year Book of Labour Statistics (1970, 1971 editions). Bulletin of Labour Statistics.

Table 8

Age Structure of Population of Europe, excluding USSR
Trends in Percentage of Population Aged 65 Years and Over

Country	Male and Female			Female		
	1950	1960	1968	1950	1960	1968
Austria[a]	10.6	13.0	13.8	11.5	14.2	16.2
Belgium[b]	10.7	12.2	13.1	11.7	13.8	15.2
Bulgaria[c]	5.8	7.2	8.5	6.1	8.0	9.6
Czechoslovakia[d]	7.6	8.5	10.4	8.3	9.7	12.2
Denmark	9.1	10.6	11.7	9.5	11.4	12.8
Finland	6.6	7.4	8.3	7.9	8.9	10.0
France[e]	11.0	11.6	12.6	12.5	14.3	15.3
Germany:						
Ger (Dem. Rep. of)	10.4	13.8[f]	15.3	10.6	15.2	17.5
Ger (Fed. Rep. of)	9.3	11.0	13.2	9.6	12.6	15.5
Greece[a]	6.7	8.2	9.6	7.3	9.1	10.6
Hungary[g]	7.5	8.2[h]	11.1	8.1	9.2	12.6
Iceland	7.5	8.1	8.6	8.6	8.9	9.4
Ireland[a]	10.7	11.2	11.2	11.1	11.8	12.2
Italy[a]	8.3	9.5	10.3[i]	8.8	10.7	11.6
Luxembourg[j]	9.4	10.8	12.2	10.1	11.9	13.8
Malta[k]	5.5	7.2	8.6	5.7	7.6	9.1
Netherlands[l]	7.0	9.0	9.9	7.2	9.5	11.0
Norway	9.6	11.1	12.7	10.6	12.2	14.2
Poland	5.2	5.9	7.9	6.1	7.0	9.2
Portugal	7.0	8.0	8.7	8.2	9.2	10.0
Rumania[m]	8.1	6.3	8.4	8.9	7.3	9.5
Spain	7.2	8.2	9.2	8.3	9.3	10.4
Sweden	10.2	12.0	13.2	10.9	13.0	14.5
Switzerland	9.6	10.2	11.3	10.6	11.9	13.0
Turkey	3.3	3.7		4.0	4.2	
United Kingdom:						
England-Wales[a]	11.0	11.9	12.6	12.6	14.3	15.3
Northern Ireland[a]	9.9	10.1	10.6	10.6	11.3	12.2
Scotland[a]	10.0	10.4	11.7	11.0	12.2	14.0
Yugoslavia[n]	5.7	6.1	7.3	6.2	7.1	8.3

[a] 1951, 1961
[b] 1947; 1961
[c] 1946, 1956, 1966
[d] 1947, 1958, 1967
[e] 1946, 1961
[f] 1966
[g] 1949, 1955

[h] 1940
[i] 1966
[j] 1947
[k] 1948
[l] 1940
[m] 1948, 1956, 1969
[n] 1948, 1961

Source: Tables 1.1a and 1.1b.   Conseil de l'Europe, 2[e] Conférence Démographique Européenne, Strasbourg, 31 août-7 septembre 1971.   Rapport sur les aspects démographiques du vieillissement de la population en Europe et ses conséquences sociales et économiques présenté par H. Darras et L. Neundörfer.

Table 9

Europe: Immigrant Wage and Salary Earners in Selected Countries

(thousands)

Immigration Country	Reference Date	Southern European						North African			Other	Citizen Immigrants	Total
		Greek	Italian	Portuguese	Spanish	Turkish	Yugoslav	Algerian	Moroccan	Tunisian			
Austria	1962[a] a.a.	0.5	1.7	-	0.2	0.2	1.0	-	-	-	2.8	-	6.5
	1971[b] a.a.	0.3	0.7	-	0.2	19.8	113.2	-	-	-	14.0	-	148.3
Belgium	1961 31 Dec	3.4	64.7	-	6.7	0.1	-	0.1	0.1	-	62.9[c]	-	138.0
	1971 a.a	7.0	85.0	3.0	30.0	11.0	-	3.0	16.0	2.0	60.0[c]	-	217.0
Denmark	1962 1 Jan	-	0.2	-	0.1	-	-		0.1[d]		10.3	-	10.6
	1972 1 Jan	-	0.6	-	0.7	5.8	4.4		1.5[d]		23.3		36.4
France	1962 7 Mar	-	267.3	28.2	192.3	-	-	196.4	19.1	11.5	232.5	28.0[f]	974.9
	1970 a.a.	4.0	235.0	190.0	256.5	4.0	33.0	245.0	60.0	30.0	142.5	100.0[g]	1 300.0
F.R. Germ	1962 30 Jun	69.1	266.0	1.4	87.3	15.3	23.6	-	3.7	0.5	188.5	-	655.5
	1972 30 Jun	269.7	422.2	63.1	184.0	497.3	471.9	1.8	13.7	10.9	382.3	-	2 317.0
Italy	1970 a.a.	0.8	-	-	0.4	1.7	0.2	3.5	-	-	32.9	-	39.5
Netherlands	1961 31 Dec	0.2	5.6	0.1	1.3	0.1	0.2	Γ	-	-	20.5[c]	29.0[h,i]	57.0
	1972[d] 15 Jun	1.1	9.5	2.5	14.8	20.9	8.8	-	14.2	-	50.4[c]	68.0[h,i]	190.3
Norway	1962 30 Sep	-	-	-	-	-	-		0.1[d]		25.5[e,k]	-	25.6
	1971 31 Aug	0.1	0.4	0.1	0.3	0.4	0.8		0.7[d]		26.7[e,k]	-	29.4
Sweden	1962 1 Apr	0.3	3.7	-	-	-	1.9	-	-	-	115.8[e,l]	-	121.7
	1972 1 Apr	8.8	4.0	-	-	-	22.9	-	-	-	182.3[e,l]	-	218.0
Switzerland	1962 Aug	-	454.4	-	44.2	-	-	-	-	-	223.1[m]	-	721.7
	1972 3rd qu	-	310.9	-	136.3	-	-	-	-	-	452.8[n]	-	900.0
United Kingdom	1961[o] 23 Apr	-	33.6	-	11.1	-	5.8		1.6[d]		517.4[p]	451.0[q]	1 020.5
	1966[r] 24 Apr	-	60.4	-	25.8	-	9.1		35.1[d]		769.0[p]	520.6[s]	1 419.7

- = Figures not available or category not applicable or magnitude negligible.

aa = Annual average.

a = Average April-December, excluding quota excess ("Kontingentüberziehungen").

b = Average April-November, including quota excess.

c = Including workers from other Benelux countries.

d = Workers from the whole of Africa.

e = Including workers from other countries of the Nordic Labour Market area.

f = Workers from the French Overseas Departments and Territories. The results of the 1962 Census for Guadeloupe and Martinique were grossed up according to their shares shown by the 1968 Census.

g = Workers from the French Overseas Departments and Territories - Estimate.

h = Excluding repatriates from Indonesian territories formerly under Netherlands administration.

i = Surinamese, Netherlands Antillians and Mollucans - 80% of all residents in 1962, 75% in 1972.

j = Excluding immigrant workers who have been employed for more than five years.

k = Of which 10 300 and 9 900 were sailors of unspecified nationality in November 1962 and November 1971, respectively.

l = Of which 51 400 and 109 200 were Finnish in 1962 and 1972, respectively.

m = Including 77 000 workers of unspecified nationality with established status.

n = Including an estimated 251 000 workers of unspecified nationality with established status, that is slightly less than 50% of all established foreign residents.

o = Economically active residents in England and Wales.

p = 180 600 aliens and 336 800 Irish in 1961; 322 100 aliens and 446 900 Irish in 1966.

q = 193 400 from Commonwealth countries (89 600 from the Caribbean area, 81 100 from India and 14 700 from Pakistan), 114 800 from Colonies and Protectorates, and 142 800 born in foreign countries and at sea.

r = Foreign born wage and salary earners resident in Great Britain, including visitors with a work place in Great Britain.

s = All Commonwealth countries, Colonies and Protectorates (179 000 from the Caribbean area, 132 200 from India and 50 500 from Pakistan).